WOK COOKBOOK

1500 Days of Simple and Delicious Recipes for Steaming, Braising, Smoking, and Stir-fry and Asian Dishes. Detailed and Suitable for Beginners and Useful for Advanced

(+4 FREE BONUS Inside Paperback Version)
+ DOWNLOAD FULL COLOR VERSION of the BOOK

Jill Yang

4 EXTRA BONUS

4 EXTRA BOOKS
MANY RECIPES
FOR
WOK & STYR FRYING
LOVERS

Scroll to the end and **SCAN** the **QR CODE** to dowload the **4 FREE eBOOKS**

Table of Contents

Introduction

A wok is typically depicted as a round, stationary cooking appliance with high edges and two or one larger handle. Food can be cooked in a shorter amount of time thanks to the wok's spherical bottom, which efficiently transfers heat. When preparing a pan fried meal, for instance, the high partitions make it easier to combine all the ingredients so that they cook at the same rate. The origins of the wok are a topic of debate amongst culinary professionals. In light of the scarcity of food in the Han period, the wok's versatility allowed for a variety of feasts to be prepared with very little components, so the theory goes. Another possible explanation is that many generations ago, when people traveled across the country carrying everything they owned, they needed a tool that could quickly prepare a large amount of food to sustain their families.

The best recipes for every meal, using common, inexpensive products and a wide range of preparation techniques, are collected in this WOK cookbook. They are healthy and simple enough for first-timers to make. Although it may seem daunting at first, making your own meals quickly becomes a satisfying and enjoyable experience. Choosing what goes into your meals is entirely up to you.

Rather than using unhealthy, processed products, you might go for organic ones. Cooking at home allows you to tailor each meal to your family's specific nutritional requirements in terms of carbohydrate, fat, protein, vitamin, and mineral intake. These days, it's common to hear that high cholesterol is to blame for people's health problems including obesity, heart disease, etc. Most people who strive to lose weight do things that are ultimately harmful to their health, such skip meals. However, if you have a wok, you may rest assured that you will start eating healthily and maintain your health.

The Chinese Wok is a good choice since it is deep and bowl-shaped, keeping your food in the center where the heat is concentrated. If this is your first time using a wok, this cookbook will introduce you to meals that are healthful, nutritious, and simple to make. First, though, we'll cover the basics of wok maintenance so you can get started cooking with your new investment. These recipes are designed to be made in an unsupervised setting at home. To make these dishes more to your liking, feel free to experiment with other ingredients and proportions. It's time to go in the kitchen and make some authentic Chinese food for yourself and your family.

Let's get started

Chapter 1: History of the Wok

Wok means "cooking tool" in its Chinese and Cantonese origin languages. Chinese historians date the wok's inception to the Han Dynasty, more than two millennia ago. Modern woks are widely available across Europe and have been modified for use on Western stoves, making this cooking tool a vital feature of Asian cuisine that can be used by anybody.

The versatility of the wok means that it may be used for cooking a wide range of dishes. The wok is an extremely versatile cooking tool that may be used for a wide variety of cooking methods, including boiling, frying, deep-frying, and steaming. So-called stir-frying is a common way to use a wok in the kitchen. It was in China some millennia ago that this most common method of preparation was developed. At this point, the wok should be very hot, and the ingredients should be added quickly while being stirred. For this reason, they only get a quick sear because they are only in the wok's searing hot base for a short period of time. The rest of the time, they cook in the wok's somewhat cooler edge, where they are constantly combined with the other ingredients thanks to the regular stirring. This style of traditional wok cooking is best performed in a round, cast-iron wok over an open fire.

Its spherical design allows for rapid cooking thanks to the wok's bottom reaching exceptionally high temperatures, making it a popular choice among chefs. The stir-frying method can be employed on European stoves even without an open fire and a spherical wok, as the high temperature on the base of the wok and the lower temperature on the sides still yields the same results. Wok cooking is a versatile, quick, and accessible method of producing a wide variety of Asian cuisine. Because of its many advantages over a traditional western pan, a wok is also a great tool for cooking Western cuisine. It's significantly quicker and more adaptable because to its unique design and substance. Due to the wok's massive heat development at its base and its high rims, food can be cooked very softly and in a fragrant aroma.

The Chinese Kitchen

There are numerous regional sub-cuisines in Chinese cuisine. Sichuan and Hunan, for example, have strong, spicy flavors, but coastal regions like Guangzhou and Shanghai have softer aromas. The usage of the wok as one of the principal cooking vessels links the cuisines of these regions. Chinese wok recipes are exceptionally well adapted to home cooking because many arose from the necessity to stretch a few ingredients far and use up tiny amounts of food. Stir-frying, in reality, makes the most of little chunks of protein.

Chinese laborers came to California in the 1860s to work on railroads. The majority were working guys who had come from rural communities outside of Canton to conduct arduous labor (now called Guangzhou). Some of these newcomers founded Chinese eateries in the hopes of providing familiar sensations from home. As a result, Chinese food in America evolved quite loosely from Cantonese cooking. Chinese immigrants all around the world have adapted classic Chinese cuisine to local food and taste preferences to create fusion gems. The immigrants were not skilled cooks, and they did not have access to the same veggies, herbs, and spices that they had in China. Instead, they had to improvise, cooking with non-Chinese vegetables like broccoli, yellow onion, pineapple, and carrot.

Stir-frying is a rapid method of cooking. Because of its architecture, the wok heats quickly and provides heat to the food practically instantly. Furthermore, by slicing proteins and vegetables into small or thin pieces, the entire dish comes together quickly - many dishes are ready in less than 10 minutes. Cooking Chinese at home is also an excellent approach to prepare nutritious meals.

You can regulate the amount of oil, salt, and sugar in your food by using your own wok and go-to recipes. These components are used liberally in professional kitchens; at home, season sparingly and taste as you go. You can also choose lean cuts of meat and load up on vegetables. Cooking tasty meals at home saves you time, money, and calories.

A wok is a multi-purpose cooking vessel that originated in China. It has a spherical bottom and is deep. Although used in other regions of the world, a wok is more widespread in China and other East and Southeast Asian countries. To answer the topic of why you should use a wok instead of a regular pan, a wok distributes heat more evenly. It might have one or two handles. Surprisingly, a wok was originally used to dry grains but is now utilized to cook stir-fry and other dishes. That's fantastic! A wok can be used for a variety of culinary techniques. Stir frying, steaming, pan frying, deep frying, braising, and poaching are some of the methods. A wok is essential for Chinese cooking. Pans and other pots cannot compete with a wok. This makes it a great piece of kitchen equipment to have if you want to enjoy a Chinese supper from the comfort of your own home. Stir frying is best done in a wok. It is available in a variety of materials, the best of which is carbon steel.

Fundamentals of the Wok

Choose the Best Wok for You

Although a good wok is essential in a family, it is best to select the suitable wok based on the type of stove you have at home. When utilizing an electric burner, for example, the type of wok you use is different than when using a gas flame stove. You can also select them according to the type of ingredient they contain. Many people like Chinese carbon steel woks because they heat and cool quickly. Consider the handles. Depending on your demands, you may like one long handle or two ear handles. Woks, on the other hand, are quite sturdy and safe, and one with a diameter of at least 12 inches is perfect for usage at home.

Clean the Wok's surface before you begin cooking.

When cooking in a wok, it's a good idea to season the surface first. As a result, your food will not cling to the surface. For example, if you're cooking chicken and it sticks to the pan, it'll burn before it's finished.

As a result, not only will the meal's flavor change, but it will also be difficult to transfer the remaining food about the wok. As a result, make your wok nonstick by pouring oil into it before cooking and draining it into a heat-resistant container once it reaches smoking temperatures. After that, add some more cooking oil to make it easier to turn and toss the meal around.

Cooking isn't limited to stir-frying.

Because it can be used for more than simply stir-frying, the wok is extremely cost-effective. Because it uses significantly less oil than a frying pan, it is great for deep frying. It can also be used to make stews, boil water, and smoke meals. Others use it to steam food, such as by inserting a bamboo steamer into the wok. Steaming can also be accomplished by placing metal trivets in the bottom of a wok, then placing a dish on top of the trivet and covering it. All of this is possible with a wok, and you may enjoy a wide range of exquisite cuisine once you learn how to make them.

Divide the Recipes

When you have recipes that require different cooking speeds, you must prepare them separately. Assume you have some meat and some crunchy vegetables, for example. Rather than cooking them all at once, consider including the vegetables near the end to get the best of both worlds. After that, add the meat and serve, as both have been properly cooked. Because of the changed timing, you won't have to worry about one being overcooked and the other being raw. Also, if you want to create extra meals, avoid repeating the recipes. It's best to repeat a process than stir-fry a large amount of food because not all of it will be scorched. Optionally, if you're cooking for a large gathering, avoid making everything a stir fry because it's time-consuming. Prepare a stew, divide the rice, and get some cold dishes ready.

Recognize the Appropriate Temperature

Assume you want to make a typical stir-fry but don't have a wok. It is best to do it on a very high heat setting. As a result, depending on the dish, increase the heat to attain the best outcomes. When making a stir fry, a little smoke or hissing isn't as bad.

Make sure your oil isn't too hot before adding your seasonings. As a result, season the wok to keep the aromatics from adhering to it rather than blending with your food. If you like chives, garlic, and other flavors, add the oil after seasoning to extract their flavor without burning when the heat is increased.

Taking Care of Your Work Is Simple

In Chinese households, the wok is a common item of cookware. As a result, they understand how to care for it appropriately. Assume this is your first time using it. To begin with, they are indestructible, so you may thoroughly clean them if necessary. However, don't forget to season it after it's clean. A scoop is superior than most instruments for removing stock water and oil as part of wok maintenance because it won't chip the wok's surface. The bamboo brush can also be used to clean plates while the food is still warm. Check that all bristles are of good quality and will not melt. When using a wok, a slotted spoon or ladles are also useful.

Using Tips for Wok

Cleaning

Cleaning the wok thoroughly after use and greasing or oiling it are also key suggestions that will allow you to enjoy your wok for a long time. As previously stated, avoid using flavor-intensive oils such as olive oil. They immediately produce bitter chemicals and smoke at the high heat of the wok.

Heating

The wok is then gradually heated to the greatest temperature. This allows the edge region to warm up because a hot wok rim is required for swirling the pan.

Oil

The wok is then filled with lard or oil, depending on the recipe. Most of the time, these will be unflavored oils like coconut, palm, or soybean oil. Olive oil has a strong flavor and begins to smoke at low temperatures, making it unsuitable for use in the wok.
In any case, the oil used should not be cold-pressed, as hazardous by-products can form when exposed to high temperatures. It would be advantageous if you ensured that the oils were refined.

Stir-Frying

The classic stir-frying technique has already been covered. This method is especially suggested since the contents in the wok are seared fast and spread around the wok by stirring movements, mixing and therefore flavoring each other. Numerous minerals, fiber, and vitamins are kept in the vegetables due to the gradual cooking on the somewhat less heated edge of the wok. As a result, wok meals stand out for their distinct nutritional value. To make traditional stir-fry correctly, all of the ingredients must be carefully cleaned and cut into pieces of the same size.

Time Adjustment

Once the fat has been heated, begin with the ingredients that require the most time to cook - these ingredients go into the wok first. Seafood, meat, and fish are examples of these. Each in small bite-sized pieces, of course. Then there are hard and soft veggies, followed by rice or pasta. These are already cooked and require the least amount of cooking time. In general, they are only momentarily heated. If required, store fish or meat on the hot wok rim to keep warm. The components are swiftly added to the wok, but the temperature must not drop due to too many ingredients being put at once. The mixture must be mixed swiftly and continuously - after all, it is called stir-frying! This keeps materials from burning on the bottom and producing bitter compounds. Because of the constant swirling, all ingredients are evenly distributed in the wok and so cooked evenly.

Versatility

Because of its versatility, the wok may be used to create a wide range of foods. With the wok, you can easily steam or fry vegetables and fish, prepare rice and soup, stew meat, mushrooms, and vegetables, fry spring rolls, and even blanch veggies. For this, a bamboo basket is preferable.

Wok Style

As previously said, there are numerous types of woks created from a wide range of materials.
Assume you're using a classic cast iron wok. In that circumstances, we recommend looking after your Asian kitchen assistant: The cast iron wok is the most effective, but owing to its material, it requires special maintenance.
Otherwise, it rusts rapidly, so wash it with water and a small amount of detergent after each use, then rub it in with a little oil. We recommend rubbing in with your hand or fingers due to the roughened surface.

Caring for Your Wok

There are a few basic things you can do to ensure that your Wok is always in prime working order. If you're just starting off, you should acquire a brand-new wok, and every fresh wok requires constant oil development until it reaches its seasoned layer. Instead of poaching everything, I recommend using the stir-fry method.

To prevent food from sticking to the Wok, heat the Wok until it is very hot before adding oil. To get started, use your peanut oil to make some delicious popcorn. You shouldn't use soap to clean your Wok; instead, rinse it with warm water after each use and wipe it off with a gentle sponge or brush.

Even though you shouldn't use abrasives or harsh objects to clean your wok, you can still wash the exterior if it gets dirty. If your WOK is brand new, you can dry it upside down after cleaning it, but if it's not, you can wipe it down—just don't leave any water behind or it might rust.

Preparing meals in a WOK and keeping it clean is much simpler than you may imagine. A seasoned layer can only form with regular use; if you can't use it that often, put some peanut oil into it and store it. You'll find a wide variety of dishes here that are perfect for using your WOK, and you'll have a great time preparing them. Keep reading as we bring you several intriguing recipes that will have you reaching for your WOK again and again.

Chapter 2: Dumpling and eggs

Basic Tofu

Preparation time: 10 minutes

Cooking Time: 15 minutes

Serving: 4

Ingredients:

1 and 1/2 teaspoons cornstarch dissolved in 1 tablespoon water

1 package (16 ounces) soft tofu, drained and cut into half-inch cubes

1 tablespoon oyster-flavored sauce

1 tablespoon soy sauce

1 tablespoon white distilled vinegar

1 teaspoon dried chili flakes

1 teaspoon garlic, minced

1 teaspoon minced ginger

1 teaspoon of sesame oil

1/2 cup chicken broth

2 tablespoons cooking oil

2 teaspoons sugar

6 ounces ground pork

Directions

In a mixing dish, combine both ground pork with oyster-flavored sauce. Allow for a 10-minute rest period. Combine the soy sauce, chicken broth, sugar, vinegar, chili flakes, and sesame oil inside a bowl to make the sauce.

Heat a wok on a high fire and add in the frying oil to cover the sides. Cook, constantly stirring, until the ginger and garlic are fragrant, approximately 10 seconds. Stir in the pork for approximately 2 minutes, or until it is lightly browned and crumbly. Bring the sauce to boil, and then remove from heat. Reduce heat to medium-low and continue to cook for another 2 minutes.

Bring the water to boil with the tofu and cook for 1 minute. Stir inside the cornstarch mixture and simmer, constantly stirring, until the sauce thickens and boils.

Nutrition: Calories 196, Fat: 16.8g, Net Carbs: 5.7g, Protein: 6.7g

Brie and Chive Omelet

Preparation time: 10 minutes

Cooking Time: 20 minutes

Serving: 4

Ingredients:

1 tablespoon fresh chives, finely chopped

1 tablespoon unsalted butter

1 teaspoon minced fresh chervil

2 ounces brie, sliced, rind discarded if preferred

3 eggs, or 2 duck eggs, beaten

Kosher salt and freshly ground black pepper

To serve:

Roasted potatoes or toast

Directions

In a wok, melt the butter on medium heat. To make huge curds, pour your eggs into the wok and stir firmly for 1 minute.

Season the eggs gently with salt and black pepper, and top with chives and chervil. 12 eggs should have Brie slices on them. Cook the omelet for another 2 minutes, or when the eggs are just set. To encapsulate the Brie-covered half, gently fold the omelet over it.

Serve over roasted potatoes, or you can toast after sliding the omelet onto a platter.

Nutrition: Calories 543.3, Fat: 47g, Net Carbs: 14.2g, Protein: 18.5g

Chive and Steamed Shrimp Dumplings

Preparation time: 10 minutes

Cooking Time: 25 minutes

Serving: 4

Ingredients:

1 1/3 cups wheat flour

1/3 cup tapioca flour

½ tablespoon salt

1 cup plus 2 tablespoons boiling water

3/4 pound raw shrimp, shelled and deveined, medium

1 cup chopped Chinese chives

1 egg white

3/4 cup bamboo shoots, finely chopped

1 tablespoon cooking oil

1 teaspoon of sesame oil

2 pinches of salt

1/8 teaspoon white pepper

2 teaspoons wine

Cabbage leaves as a lining for the dumplings

Directions

To make the wrappers, whisk together the wheat flour, tapioca flour, and salt in a mixing dish. Stir in boiling water using a wooden spoon and chopsticks until the bowl's side is clean. Cover and set aside for 5 minutes to cool. Knead the dough once it has cooled enough to handle until it is smooth and free of lumps. The dough mustn't cling to your hands. Cover and set aside until prepared to use.

Prepare the filling as follows: Chop the shrimp coarsely and combine with the chives, egg white, bamboo shoots, salt, wine, sesame oil, and white pepper in a mixing bowl; toss well.

Cut dough into four equal pieces. To keep the other pieces from drying out, work on one portion at a time. Cut each portion into pieces by rolling it into a half-inch cylinder. Make spherical circles out of the components. Roll all circles into 3–3 and half-inch circles using a rolling pin.

To wrap, put a rounded spoonful of filling into the dough's middle. To make a semicircle, fold your dough over the filling. To seal all edges, pinch them together. While forming the leftover dumplings, cover with a moist towel.

Prepare a steaming wok. The cabbage leaves should be used to scrape the base of a steamer. Set the dumplings just on leaves in an orderly manner. Cover and steam for 8 minutes, or till the dumplings are transparent.

Serve cooked dumplings hot with your favorite dipping sauce.

Nutrition: Calories 130, Fat: 2g, Net Carbs: 18g, Protein: 9

Puffs Along With Three-Color Vegetables

Preparation time: 10 minutes

Cooking Time: 25 minutes

Serving: 4

Ingredients:

1 tablespoon cooking oil

1 cup snap sugar peas, stem ends snapped off, and fibrous strings removed

8 tofu puffs

1/2 cup All-Purpose Stir-Fry Sauce

1/2 cup water chestnuts

1/2 cup shelled hardboiled quail eggs or canned quail eggs (optional)

1/4 cup water

3/4 cup thinly sliced carrots

Directions

In a mixing bowl, combine the Stir-Fry Sauce and water.

Heat a wok on a high fire and add in the oil to cover the sides.

Stir in the carrots and snap sugar peas for approximately 1 minute or until the veggies are soft crisp. Stir in the tofu puffs and water chestnuts for 1 minute.

Add sauce and the quail eggs, if preferred. Reduce heat to medium-low and cook for 3 minutes, covered.

Nutrition: Calories 130, Fat: 9g, Net Carbs: 2g, Protein: 11g

Tofu With Cashews and Mushrooms

Preparation time: 10 minutes

Cooking Time: 25 minutes

Serving: 4

Ingredients:

1 package (16 ounces) regular tofu, drained, dried well, and cut into half-inch cubes

1 tablespoon hoisin sauce

1 teaspoon garlic, minced

1 teaspoon of sesame oil

1/2 cup chicken broth

1/2 cup roasted cashews

2 teaspoons soy sauce

6 asparagus spears, cut at an angle into 1-inch pieces

6 medium white button mushrooms, quartered

Cooking oil for deep-frying

Directions

Combine some chicken broth, soy sauce, hoisin sauce, and sesame oil inside a bowl to make the sauce. Heat the deep-frying oil in a wok. Deep-fry your tofu, some few pieces at a time, until golden brown and crisp, approximately 2 minutes per side. Drain on paper towels after removing with a slotted spoon.

Heat a wok on a high fire and add in 1 spoonful of the oil to cover the sides. Cook, constantly stirring, until the garlic is aromatic, approximately 10 seconds. Toss in the asparagus and cook for 30 seconds. Cook about 1 minute after adding the mushrooms.

Toss in the tofu and the sauce. Bring to a boil, and then reduce the sauce somewhat.

Stir in the cashews to cover them.

Nutrition: Calories 287, Fat: 26.3g, Net Carbs: 15g, Protein: 26.3g

Shrimp with tofu

Preparation time: 10 minutes

Cooking Time: 20 minutes

Serving: 4

Ingredients:

6 ounces medium raw shrimp, shelled and deveined

1 teaspoon of cornstarch dissolved in 2 teaspoons water

1 and 1/2 teaspoons hoisin sauce

1 package (16 ounces) firm tofu, drained, and cut into half-inch cubes

1 tablespoon Chinese rice wine

1 tablespoon cooking oil

1 teaspoon of cornstarch

1 teaspoon of sesame oil

1/2 cup frozen peas, thawed

1/3 cup chicken broth

2 teaspoons chili garlic sauce

4 pieces thinly sliced ginger

Directions

Combine whole shrimp and cornstarch; toss to cover. Allow for a 10-minute rest period.

Combine the rice wine, chicken broth, chili garlic sauce, hoisin sauce, and sesame oil inside a bowl to make the sauce.

Heat a wok on a high fire and add in the frying oil to cover the sides. Cook, constantly stirring, until the ginger is aromatic, approximately 10 seconds. Stir in the shrimp for approximately half a minute or until they become slightly pink. Stir in the peas and cook for a further minute.

Add the tofu and gently stir for 1 minute. Bring the sauce to boil, and then remove from the heat. Stir inside cornstarch solution and simmer, constantly stirring, until the sauce thickens and boils.

Nutrition: Calories 220, Fat: 8g, Net Carbs: 3g, Protein: 28g

Tomato Eggs

Preparation time: 10 minutes

Cooking Time: 25 minutes

Serving: 4

Ingredients:

2 tablespoons of soy sauce

2 teaspoons packed brown sugar

2 teaspoons chili garlic sauce

5 eggs, lightly beaten

1 green onion, thinly sliced

2 medium tomatoes, peeled, seeded, and cut into one-inch cubes

2 1/2 tablespoons cooking oil

1/4 cup chicken broth

1/4 cup ketchup

Directions

Combine the ketchup, chicken broth, brown sugar, soy sauce, and chili garlic sauce in a bowl to make the sauce.

Heat a wok on a high fire and add in the oil to cover all sides.

Stir in the green onion, eggs, and tomatoes for about 1 minute, or until the eggs are slightly set.

Add the sauce and stir for 1 minute to combine.

Nutrition: Calories 237.8, Fat: 16.3g, Net Carbs: 7.1g, Protein: 16.3g

Egg and Scallion Dumplings

Preparation time: 10 minutes

Cooking Time: 25 minutes

Serving: 4

Ingredients:

½ teaspoon toasted sesame oil

1 teaspoon garlic, minced

2 scallions, trimmed and chopped

2 tablespoons vegetable or peanut oil

24 to 30 dumpling, gyoza, or potsticker wrappers

4 large eggs, beaten

Freshly ground black pepper

Sea salt

Directions

Add both veggie oil and sesame oil to a heated wok. Cook for approximately half a minute after adding the garlic.

Season the eggs with sea salt and pepper before adding them to the wok. With a heat-proof spatula, scramble the eggs for approximately half a minute or till done. Combine the scallions and scrambled eggs in a mixing bowl. Place the eggs on a platter and put them away to cool until you can handle them.

Fill the middle of the dumpling wrapper with a heaping spoonful of an egg and scallion mixture. Wet all edges of the wrapper using water, fold into the wrapper to cover the filling and then crimp the wrapper at the corners to seal the dumpling.

Using the leftover wrappers and filling, repeat the process. Ensure that uncooked dumplings do not come into contact with one another. They'll stay together until they're ready to eat.

Dumplings may be steamed, pan-fried, broiled, deep-fried, or used in soup.

Nutrition: Calories 45, Fat: 2g, Net Carbs: 4g, Protein: 1

Marbled Tea Eggs

Preparation time: 10 minutes

Cooking Time: 30 minutes

Serving: 4

Ingredients:

½ cup soy sauce

1 cinnamon stick

2 black tea bags

2 pieces star anise

2 teaspoons sugar

2 thin strips of orange peel

8 eggs

Directions

Cover all eggs with water in a medium wok. Bring your water to a simmer, then reduce to low heat and keep it there. Cook for approximately 10 minutes, or until the eggs are hard-boiled.

Cool the eggs over cold running water after removing them from the wok. Crack all eggs evenly all over by using the back of the spoon, being careful not to take off the shells.

Add all tea bags, sugar, soy sauce, star anise, orange peel, and cinnamon stick to the wok with the eggs. Fill the wok halfway with water to cover your eggs.

Bring your water to a boil, and then reduce heat to low. Cook the eggs for about 40 minutes on low heat.

Allow the eggs to soak for a minimum of 1 hour after turning off the heat and covering the wok with a lid.

The taste and color of the eggs will get stronger the longer they are steeped.

The eggs should be drained. Serve as a snack or alongside noodles or rice right away.

Nutrition: Calories 79, Fat: 4.4g, Net Carbs: 3.3g, Protein: 6.8g

Rancheros with Two Salsas

Preparation time: 10 minutes

Cooking Time: 45 minutes

Serving: 4

Ingredients:

1 and 1/2 cups Tomato Salsa

1 ripe Hass avocado, pitted, peeled, and diced

1 tablespoon veggie oil, or more as needed

2 cups cooked black beans, seasoned with 1 minced jalapeño, chili, 1 garlic, minced clove, 1 teaspoon ground coriander, and salt

2 cups shredded Monterey jack or cheddar cheese

2 tablespoons of fresh cilantro, chopped

2 tablespoons El Yucateco or other green hot sauce

5 scallions, chopped

8 (6-inch) corn tortillas

8 eggs

Directions

Preheat the wok.

Remove the beans from heat and put them aside. Make the green salsa with the avocado, cilantro, scallions, and spicy sauce; leave aside.

In a large wok, heat oil. Warm each tortilla in the heated oil for a few seconds on each side, just enough to soften and heat through. To drain, place on paper towels.

Cook the eggs in any way you like. Place two tortillas side by side on every serving platter while they're cooking. Place a dollop of beans on every tortilla, then a slice of cheese over the beans, and broil the dishes to melt all cheese. Place an egg and a spoonful of green salsa; on the other, place a spoonful of Tomato Salsa. Serve right away.
Nutrition: Calories 251.4, Fat: 9.2g, Net Carbs: 34.1g, Protein: 11.2g

Green Eggs and Ham

Preparation time: 10 minutes
Cooking Time: 25 minutes
Serving: 4
Ingredients:
1 tablespoon green hot sauce
1/2 teaspoon salt
1/3 cup milk
1/4 cup maple syrup
2 tablespoons butter
2 tablespoons chopped fresh flat-leaf parsley
2 tablespoons red hot sauce
3 scallions, chopped
4 slices ham (1/4 inch thick)
8 large eggs
Freshly ground black pepper
Directions
Preheat the wok.
In a wok, place the ham. Pour the maple syrup with red hot sauce over the ham and mix well.
Whisk the eggs, salt, milk, and pepper to taste in a large mixing bowl. Combine the parsley, scallions, and green hot sauce in a blender and mix until smooth.
Melt the butter on medium heat in a large wok before adding the eggs. While you're scrambling the eggs, brown the ham on both sides by flipping it once. Spoon a few ham extracts onto each dish before topping with ham and eggs.
Nutrition: Calories 220, Fat: 13.8g, Net Carbs: 5g, Protein: 18.6g

Chilies Rellenos

Preparation time: 10 minutes

Cooking Time: 25 minutes

Serving: 4

Ingredients:

1 1/2 pounds fresh poblano chilies

1 3/4 cups shredded cheddar or Mexican blend cheese

1/2 teaspoon salt

1/4 cup unbleached all-flour

2/3 cup whole milk

3 eggs

Freshly ground black pepper

Directions

Preheat your wok.

Place the chilies on a wok in a thin layer and broil until charred on both sides, rotating once or twice to ensure equal cooking. Wrap all chilies in foil and set them aside to steam for 10–15 minutes. Remove any charred skin and stalks, then cut the fruit half lengthwise and scoop the seeds out. Allow airing to dry.

Reduce the cooking temperature. Grease 1 8-inch wok lightly. In the base of the pot, equally, distribute the chilies. 1 cup of cheese should be sprinkled on top. Add the rest of the chilies halves on top.

Combine the eggs, flour, milk, salt, and pepper in a blender or mixing bowl. Pour the sauce over the chilies. Sprinkle the leftover 3/4 cup of grated cheese on top. Cook for 25–30 minutes, covered with foil. Remove foil and cook for another 5–10 minutes, or until the filling is barely set. Allow for a 5-minute rest period before serving.

Nutrition: Calories 350, Fat: 18g, Net Carbs: 27g, Protein: 22g

Chapter 3: Vegetables Recipes

Shredded Potatoes in Scallions

Preparation time: 10 minutes

Cooking time: 25 minutes

Serving:4

Ingredients:

1 tablespoon black vinegar

1 tablespoon soy sauce

2 medium low-starch potatoes (such as red-skinned potatoes), scrubbed

2 or 3 garlic cloves, crushed

2 scallions, thinly sliced

2 whole dried chilies (optional)

3 tablespoons peanut or vegetable oil

Directions

Cut all potatoes into matchsticks, ensuring they are all the same size.

To eliminate part of the starch from the potato shreds, soak them in chilly water for 10 minutes. Then wash, rinse, and dry them completely.

Heat your peanut oil inside a hot wok on high fire until it begins to smoke. Stir in the garlic and chilies (if using) for another 15 seconds. Stir in the scallions for approximately half a minute before they start to burn.

Stir-fry the potatoes for 2–3 minutes in the wok. Then throw in the black vinegar to mix everything. Stir in the soy sauce for another 2–3 minutes, or till the potatoes are fully cooked.

Nutrition: Calories 40, Fat: 1.5g, Net Carbs: 5g, Protein: 1g

Chinese Broccoli with a Simple Seasoning

Preparation time: 10 minutes

Cooking time: 30 minutes

Serving:4

Ingredients:

1 pound Chinese broccoli (Gai Lan), washed and trimmed

1 tablespoon oyster sauce

1 teaspoon of sesame oil

2 garlic cloves, thinly sliced

2 tablespoons peanut oil

2 tablespoons of soy sauce

Directions

In a wok, bring 1 cup of water to boil.

Heat the wok on high fire till drops of water sizzle when it comes into contact.

Cook for around 15 seconds after adding the oil and garlic to the pan.

Stir-fry the Chinese broccoli quickly in the garlic oil.

Cook for 5–6 minutes, or when the broccoli is tender-crisp, in half a cup of boiling water in the wok.

Add the soy or oyster sauces to a wok and stir-fry for 1 minute to mix with the broccoli.

Take the wok off the heat and drizzle in the sesame oil.

Combine all ingredients in a mixing bowl and serve.

Nutrition: Calories 22, Fat: 0.7g, Net Carbs: 3.8g, Protein: 1.1g

Garlic and Ginger Pea Shoots

Preparation time: 10 minutes

Cooking time: 20 minutes

Serving:4

Ingredients:

1 pound (500 grams) fresh Chinese pea shoots or spinach

2 slices fresh ginger, thinly sliced

2 tablespoons oil

3 cloves of garlic, minced

Sauce

1 teaspoon of salt

1 teaspoon sugar

1/2 teaspoon ground Sichuan pepper

2 teaspoons rice wine

2 teaspoons of sesame oil

Directions

Carefully wash and drain the pea shoots. Discard wilted or yellowing leaves, as well as stiff stems. Set aside. Set aside the ingredients for the sauce.

In a wok, heat oil; then add the ginger and garlic and stir-fry briskly for half a minute to release the scents.

Add the pea shoots and stir-fry for approximately 3 minutes, or till the leaves become a deeper green, rotating multiple times to cover equally with oil.

Add all the sauce and stir-fry for another 3 minutes, or till the leaves become a darker green. Transfer to a serving plate and serve right away.

Nutrition: Calories 170.7, Fat: 1.7g, Net Carbs: 6.4g, Protein: 13.9g

Garlic Bok Choy

Preparation time: 10 minutes

Cooking time: 20 minutes

Serving:4

Ingredients:

¼ teaspoon ground ginger

½ teaspoon toasted sesame oil

1 or 2 garlic cloves, minced

1½ pounds baby bok Choy

1½ tablespoons peanut or vegetable oil

3 tablespoons vegetable broth

Sea salt

Directions

Trim the baby bok Choy's root ends. The leaves should be well washed and drained.

Heat the peanut oil in a wok on medium to high heat, spread it around to cover the whole wok.

Cook for 30–60 seconds after adding the garlic and ginger. Don't let them become too hot. Add fresh bok Choy leaves after the spices have gotten aromatic. Stir everything up until everything is properly incorporated. In a wok, add the vegetable broth. Cook for 1 minute with the lid on the wok. Turn the heat down and remove the lid from the wok. Toss the bok Choy along a pinch of sea salt and a spritz of sesame oil to cover. Serve right away.

Nutrition: Calories 9, Fat: 0.67g, Net Carbs: 1.5g, Protein: 1.1g

Green Beans Dry-Fried

Preparation time: 10 minutes

Cooking time: 20 minutes

Serving:4

Ingredients:

¼ cup peanut or vegetable oil

1 garlic clove, crushed

1 pound string beans, trimmed and completely dry

1 teaspoon Shaoxing rice wine

2 tablespoons oyster sauce

3 scallions, thinly sliced

Directions

Preheat the wok at a high flame. Add your peanut oil once it is heated. Cook the string beans in the wok till they are scratchy and blistered, approximately 5 minutes, turning them constantly. Take the beans out of the wok.

Stir-fry the smashed garlic, rice wine, oyster sauce, and scallions in the wok on high heat for approximately half a minute or aromatic.

Add the beans to the wok and toss them inside the sauce until they're well covered. For 1 minute, stir-fry the beans. Serve.

Nutrition: Calories 340, Fat: 28g, Net Carbs: 3g, Protein: 17g

Mixed Vegetables

Preparation time: 10 minutes

Cooking time: 60 minutes

Serving:4

Ingredients:

1 cup (5 ounce/150 grams) fresh or frozen peas

1 bell pepper, diced

2 carrots, diced

8 ounces (250 grams) fresh or frozen corn kernels (about 1 and 1/2 cups)

5 ounces (150 grams) green beans, ends and strings removed, diced

1-inch fresh ginger, minced

1 onion, diced

1 teaspoon Sichuan Pepper-Salt Powder

2 tablespoons oil

Sauce

1 tablespoon soy sauce

1 tablespoon water

1 teaspoon of sesame oil

1 teaspoon sugar

1/2 teaspoon salt

Directions

When using fresh peas, remove them from their pods; if using frozen peas, thaw them.

In a small dish, mix the sauce ingredients and put them aside.

In a wok, heat oil and stir-fry the carrot, corn, bell pepper, green beans, onion, and ginger for about 2 minutes once it is hot.

Cook for another 1–2 minutes after adding the peas.

Reduce heat to low, simmer for approximately 3 minutes, then whisk inside the Sichuan Pepper-Salt. Blend for 1 minute longer to properly integrate the flavors. Serve right away.

Nutrition: Calories 160, Fat: 2g, Net Carbs: 26g, Protein: 2g

Napa Cabbage in Tofu Skins

Preparation time: 10 minutes

Cooking time: 40 minutes

Serving:4

Ingredients:

1 sheet dried tofu skin (about 2 1/2 ounces/80 grams), soaked in water for 10 minutes, then drained

1 tablespoon sesame oil

12 ounces (350 grams) Chinese or Napa cabbage

2 tablespoons oil

4 slices fresh ginger, thinly sliced

Sauce

1 tablespoon soy sauce

1 teaspoon rice wine

1 teaspoon of salt

1 teaspoon sugar

1 teaspoon vinegar

Directions

Cut the cabbage leaves into similar-sized pieces. The tofu skin should be cut into tiny pieces.

Place all of the sauce ingredients in a mixing bowl and set aside.

Warm oil in a wok until it is hot but not burning.

Stir-fry for approximately 1 minute with the tofu peel. Stir in the ginger and cabbage for another 3 to 4 minutes or till the cabbage is soft.

Reduce your heat to low and simmer for 1–2 minutes after adding the sauce mixture.

Serve in a serving dish.

Nutrition: Calories 164, Fat: 11g, Net Carbs: 12g, Protein: 4g

Peanuts and Chili in Tofu and Green Beans

Preparation time: 10 minutes

Cooking time: 20 minutes

Serving:4

Ingredients:

1 tablespoon sesame oil

2 tablespoons oil

1 block (10 ounce/300 grams) pressed or firm tofu, cut into cubes

2 to 3 green onions (scallions), cut into sections

2 to 4 red finger-length chilies, deseeded and then sliced

10 ounces (300 grams) green beans, strings removed

6 to 8 garlic cloves, minced

1-inch fresh ginger, minced

1 cup roasted unsalted peanuts, skins removed

Sauce

1 tablespoon rice wine

1 tablespoon soy sauce

1 teaspoon of sesame oil

1 teaspoon sugar

1/2 teaspoon salt

Directions

In a small dish, combine the sauce ingredients and put them aside.

Heat both oils on medium heat in a wok, and then add tofu and chilies. Stir-fry until 1 minute before adding the green beans, ginger, and garlic, and continue to stir-fry for another 1 to 2 minutes.

Stir-fry until 2 minutes with the peanuts and sauce combination.

Transfer to a bowl after stirring in the green onions.

Nutrition: Calories 179.3, Fat: 7.7g, Net Carbs: 13.6g, Protein: 11.2g

Sichuan Meat Sauce in Fried Eggplant

Preparation time: 10 minutes

Cooking time: 20 minutes

Serving:4

Ingredients:

4 slender Asian eggplants, cut in half, then quartered lengthwise

8 slices fresh ginger, minced

6 garlic cloves, minced

1/2 cup (4 ounce/100 grams) ground pork, beef, or chicken

1 tablespoon black bean chili paste

1/2 cup (125 milliliters) plus 2 tablespoons oil

6 green onions (scallions), minced

Sauce

1 tablespoon sugar, or more to taste

1 teaspoon of salt

1 teaspoon of sesame oil

1 teaspoon vinegar

1/2 teaspoon freshly ground black pepper

2 tablespoons of water

2 teaspoons rice wine

2 teaspoons soy sauce

Directions

Set aside the ingredients for the sauce.

In a wok, heat half a cup of oil over high fire and then add the eggplants. Stir-fry until they soften and change color, stirring regularly. Remove the eggplants from the wok and drain them on a rack or in a colander.

Heat the remaining 2 tablespoons of oil until it reaches a high temperature. Stir-fry for 1 minute with the garlic and ginger. Stir in the ground beef and cook for another 2 minutes. Stir in the black bean chili paste for another 30 seconds. Stir in the sauce mixture to combine all of the ingredients.

Stir in the cooked eggplants until they are well covered. Cover and cook for approximately 3 minutes, or until the vegetables are soft and aromatic. Transfer to a serving plate and top with green onions, minced.

Nutrition: Calories 324, Fat: 2.4g, Net Carbs: 29.8g, Protein: 15.4g

Sour and Sweet Eggplant

Preparation time: 10 minutes

Cooking time: 20 minutes

Serving:4

Ingredients:

4 slender Asian eggplants, about 1 1/3 pounds

1 cup oil

5 cardamom pods

5 whole cloves

2 green finger-length chilies split lengthwise

1 tablespoon ground fennel

1/2 teaspoon of cumin, ground

1/2 teaspoon ground turmeric

2 teaspoons ground red pepper

1 teaspoon garam masala

3 heaping tablespoons tamarind pulp soaked in 1 and 1/2 cups water, mashed, and strained to obtain the extract

4 tablespoons caster sugar

Salt to taste

Directions

Cut the eggplants lengthwise into quarters and 1 and a half-inch length.

In a wok, heat oil and fry all eggplants until half-cooked. Drain the water and put it aside.

Discard all the oil except 2 tablespoons. Fry until fragrant the cloves, cardamom pods, and green chilies.

Add the fried eggplant, ground spice powders, salt, and sugar, as well as the tamarind extract. Heat until the eggplant is cooked and the sauce has thickened.

Nutrition: Calories 70, Fat: 1g, Net Carbs: 13g, Protein: 3g

Spicy Garlic Eggplant

Preparation time: 10 minutes

Cooking time: 20 minutes

Serving:4

Ingredients:

¼ cup chicken broth

1 tablespoon brown sugar

1 tablespoon chili oil

1 tablespoon Chinese black vinegar or good balsamic vinegar

¼ teaspoon red pepper flakes

1 tablespoon soy sauce

1 tablespoon fresh minced ginger

2 garlic cloves, minced

2 scallions, minced

2 tablespoons peanut or vegetable oil

2 to 3 Asian eggplants, cut into thin, 1-inch-long strips

Directions

Combine the chicken broth, vinegar, soy sauce, brown sugar, chili oil, and red pepper flakes in a small bowl. Set aside.

Heat a wok at a high temperature till one drop of water sputters as it comes into contact with it. Add in the peanut oil to cover your wok.

Add all eggplants to the wok to stir-fry for 2–3 minutes, or until golden brown on the outsides. Reduce to medium-high heat and stir in the scallions, garlic, and ginger. Stir-fry for approximately half a minute before adding this chicken broth mix and tossing the veggies until well-coated.

Allow the veggies to absorb your sauce for 2–3 minutes before serving.

Nutrition: Calories 520, Fat: 16.6g, Net Carbs: 68.8g, Protein: 15.4g

Steamed Chinese Eggs

Preparation time: 10 minutes

Cooking time: 25 minutes

Serving:4

Ingredients:

1 cup water

1 scallion, finely chopped

2 teaspoons sea salt

3 medium eggs

Sesame oil

Soy sauce

Directions

In a large mixing bowl, whisk together the eggs. Using a strainer, strain the eggs into a steam-proof dish. In a separate bowl, mix the eggs and the sea salt.

Bring your water to boil in a wok over high heat.

In the wok, place a steam rack or a colander with legs. Carefully lay the egg-filled dish in the wok and cover it with a heat-resistant plate. Reduce to a low heat setting and steam your eggs for 15 minutes.

Remove the dish with care. Serve your eggs with soy sauce, sesame oil, and a sliced scallion on top.

Nutrition: Calories 124.6, Fat: 5.5g, Net Carbs: 2.6g, Protein: 11.7g

Stir-Fry Spinach and Black Bean Sauce

Preparation time: 10 minutes

Cooking time: 18 minutes

Serving:4

Ingredients:

1 pound (500 grams) water spinach or regular spinach, tough stems discarded, carefully washed, and snipped into sections

1 red finger-length chili, deseeded and sliced (optional)

1 tablespoon black bean paste (tau cheo)

2 tablespoons oil

3 cloves of garlic, minced

Directions

In a wok, heat the oil until it is extremely hot, and then stir-fry the garlic with black bean paste for approximately 30 seconds.

Turn down the heat to moderate and stir-fry water spinach with red chili for approximately 3 minutes, or till wilted and all bean paste is equally distributed.

Take the wok off the heat, and then serve.

Nutrition: Calories 70, Fat: 3.8g, Net Carbs: 6.1g, Protein: 1.5g

Tomatoes With Onion in Pine Nuts

Preparation time: 10 minutes

Cooking time: 20 minutes

Serving:4

Ingredients:

1/3 cup (2 ounce/50 grams) pine nuts

1 large onion, diced

2 green onions (scallions) cut into lengths

3 large ripe tomatoes cut into wedges

1 teaspoon of soy sauce

1 teaspoon sugar

1/3 teaspoon salt

2 tablespoons oil

Fresh coriander leaves (cilantro) to garnish

Directions

Dry-roast your pine nuts in a dry wok on medium-low heat, turning regularly, for approximately 3 to 4 minutes, or until golden brown. Remove the wok from heat and put it aside.

Heat oil in a wok at high temperature until it shimmers, and then stir-fries all onions and green onions for half a minute to release the fragrances.

Stir in the tomatoes, salt, pine nuts, sugar, and soy sauce for 1–2 minutes, stirring constantly. Remove the wok from heat, add the coriander leaves, and then serve right away.

Nutrition: Calories 270, Fat: 27g, Net Carbs: 8g, Protein: 3g

Chapter 4: Fish and seafood's Recipes

Chili Bean Sauce Shrimp

Preparation time: 10 minutes

Cooking Time: 28 minutes

Serving: 4

Ingredients:

1 pound large shrimp, peeled and deveined

1 tablespoon minced mild fresh chilies, seeded

1 tablespoon of salt

1 teaspoon chili bean sauce

2 tablespoons chopped scallions

2 tablespoons minced ginger

2 tablespoons Shao Hsing rice wine

2 tablespoons of soy sauce

3 tablespoons vegetable oil

Few cilantro sprigs

1/2 teaspoon sugar

Directions

Combine the salt and 3 cups of chilled water in a large mixing bowl. Allow 1 hour for the shrimp to soak. Using multiple sheets of paper towels, drain the shrimp. Pat, the shrimp dry with extra paper towels. Combine soy sauce, sugar, and chili bean sauce in a small bowl.

Over a high fire, heat a plain wok until a drop of water sputters within 1–2 seconds of touch. Add in 2 tablespoons of oil, then the shrimp, and stir-fry for 1 minute, or until they become no pink. Add rice wine and remove your wok from heat right away. Place it on a platter to cool. Stir the leftover 1 tablespoon of oil into the wok on high heat for 5 seconds before adding the ginger, chilies, and scallions. Add your soy sauce mixture and stir it around. Return your shrimp to the wok and stir-fry for half a minute–1 minute, or until cooked through. Serve with cilantro sprigs as a garnish.

Nutrition: Calories 231.6, Fat: 1.7g, Net Carbs: 29.8g, Protein: 25g

Clams in a Sauce of Black Beans

Preparation time: 10 minutes

Cooking Time: 35 minutes

Serving:

Ingredients:

¼ cup room temperature water

¼ small sweet onion, chopped

1 tablespoon peanut or vegetable oil

1 teaspoon black bean sauce

1 teaspoon fresh chopped ginger

1 teaspoon Shaoxing rice wine

1 teaspoon sugar

1½ pounds littleneck or Manila clams, scrubbed and rinsed well

2 dried red chilies

3 garlic cloves, minced

Directions

Discard any littleneck clams with damaged shells or already opened. If they seem gritty, soak the clams in salty water for 1–2 hours. Before cooking, give them another rinse.

Heat the peanut oil in a wok at high flame till a droplet of water sputters on contact. Toss for approximately half a minute after adding the garlic, ginger, onion, and chilies.

In a wok, combine all black bean sauce with water. To blend, stir everything together. Then add the clams, sugar, and rice wine. Bring the liquid to boil, cover the wok and wait for the clams to open.

Serve over rice or noodles as a side dish.

Nutrition: Calories 280, Fat: 12.2g, Net Carbs: 30.5g, Protein: 6.7g

Crabs in Black Bean Sauce

Preparation time: 10 minutes

Cooking Time: 25 minutes

Serving: 4

Ingredients:

1 large egg, beaten

1 tablespoon fermented black beans, rinsed

1 tablespoon soy sauce

1 teaspoon of cornstarch

1/3 cup Homemade Chicken Broth

1/4 teaspoon of white pepper, ground

2 scallions, cut into 2-inch pieces

2 tablespoons ground pork

2 tablespoons vegetable oil

4 live blue crabs (about 2 pounds)

4 slices ginger

1/2 teaspoon salt

Directions

Place the crabs inside a bag and freeze for approximately an hour, or till all crabs are no more active. Twist off the apron and place every crab shell piece down on a chopping board. Remove both sides of the spongy gills by removing the hard shell. With a cleaver, remove little legs and discard them. Each crab should be cut in half. Rinse the crabs in chilled water in a colander. Excess water should be shaken off. Chop all black beans coarsely. Combine the cornstarch and 2 tablespoons of cool water in a small bowl. Set aside.

Over a high fire, heat a plain wok until a drop of water sputters within 1–2 seconds of touch. Stir in the oil, then add your ginger and only the white portion of the scallions, stirring for 10 seconds or till fragrant. Stir in the black beans for 10 seconds. Stir-fry the pork for approximately 20 seconds, or till it is no pinker. Stir-fry the half crabs for 20 seconds. Cook, covered, for 3 to 4 minutes, or when the crabs start to turn orange, tossing halfway through. Stir in the soy sauce, salt, and pepper, as well as the remaining scallion greens. Cook for 1 minute with the lid on. Stir together the cornstarch and water then pour it into a wok alongside the egg. Stir-fry for half a minute or till the crabs are barely cooked.

Nutrition: Calories 27, Fat: 0.3g, Net Carbs: 5.1g, Protein: 0.8g

Fennel and Dill in Steamed Salmon

Preparation time: 10 minutes

Cooking Time: 55 minutes

Serving: 4

Ingredients:

For the salmon:

3 tablespoons dry white wine

Kosher salt and freshly ground black pepper

Two 1-pound wild salmon fillets, cut into 4 equal portions

For the fennel and dill Salad:

¼ cup freshly squeezed lemon extract (from 2 medium lemons)

⅓ cup olive oil

⅓ cup shelled pistachios

½ cup crumbled feta or goat cheese

1 tablespoon honey

2 medium fennel bulbs, trimmed and shaved into paper-thin slices

3 tablespoons fresh dill, finely chopped

Kosher salt and freshly ground black pepper

Directions

Place the salmon in a shallow, microwave-safe dish or bowl to cook. Season to taste with pepper and salt before pouring the wine on it.

In the base of a wok, pour approximately one inch of water and place a steamer rack. Bring to a boil on high heat, then place the fishbowl on the rack and reduce heat on medium to keep the water at a low simmer. Cover the fish and steam it for 10–12 minutes. Preserve an eye on the water level and add additional if necessary to keep the wok from drying out. With a fork, check for doneness; the fish must be moist and starting to flake.

Whisk the lemon, oil, and honey in a mixing bowl to make the Salad Prep. Drizzle as much topping over the fennel as desired, then mix with pistachios, dill, and cheese. Season with pepper and salt to taste.

Place a slice of salmon and a bit of the Salad Prep on each dish to serve.

Nutrition: Calories 316, Fat: 28g, Net Carbs: 3.9g, Protein: 23.9g

Fish Sliced in a Delicious Black Bean Sauce

Preparation time: 10 minutes

Cooking Time: 20 minutes

Serving: 4

Ingredients:

1 1/2 pounds (700 grams) fish steaks or fillets

1 1/2 to 2 tablespoons black bean paste (tau cheo)

1 teaspoon coarsely ground black pepper

1 teaspoon sugar

2 sprigs fresh coriander leaves (cilantro), minced, as garnish (optional)

3 tablespoons oil

3–4 garlic cloves, minced

6 green onions (scallions), cut into sections

Marinade:

1 teaspoon of sesame oil

2 tablespoons rice wine

3 tablespoons fresh ginger, minced

Directions

Cut the fish into small pieces. Remove bones from the steaks if you're using them. In a mixing bowl, place the fish.

Combine the ingredients for the marinade, pour on the fish, and flip to cover evenly. Cover and leave aside for 30 minutes to marinate.

Heat oil in a wok on high heat and add marinated fish with garlic. Stir-fry for 1–2 minutes, or until the color of the fish changes. Cook for 1 to 2 minutes after adding the black bean paste.

Stir in the sugar, green onions, and roughly powdered black pepper for another minute to incorporate the flavors. Serve in a serving dish.

Nutrition: Calories 300, Fat: 15g, Net Carbs: 6g, Protein: 31g

Fried Rice with Shrimp and Egg

Preparation time: 10 minutes

Cooking Time: 03 minutes

Serving: 2

Ingredients:

½ cup frozen peas

½ Pound medium-size shrimp, peeled and deveined

½ teaspoon of kosher salt

1 teaspoon of cornstarch

1 teaspoon of sesame oil

2 teaspoons ginger, freshly grated

2 to 3 teaspoons of soy sauce

3 cups day-old cooked long-grain white rice

3 eggs, beaten

3 scallions, finely chopped

4 tablespoons vegetable oil, divided

Directions

Toss the shrimp, cornstarch, and salt, in a small basin and set aside for 10 minutes.

In a wok, heat 2 tablespoons of the oil over a high flame. Fry the shrimp until they just start to turn opaque on both sides, approximately 1 minute on each side. Take the shrimp out of the wok and put them aside.

In the same wok, add the rest of 2 teaspoons of oil. Fry the scallions, ginger, and eggs for less than 1 minute, or till the yolks are still flowing but starting to set. Add rice and simmer, constantly stirring, until the egg is broken up into little bits that adhere to the rice.

Toss inside the frozen peas, then season with soy sauce to suit. Continue to cook the rice until it is piping hot. Cook for a further minute after adding the shrimp. Serve with a drizzle of sesame oil on top.

Nutrition: Calories 224.9, Fat: 4.8g, Net Carbs: 29.2g, Protein: 16.5g

Garlic Shrimp from Vietnam

Preparation time: 10 minutes

Cooking Time: 40 minutes

Serving: 4

Ingredients:

1 1/2 pounds (700 grams) fresh shrimp, peeled and deveined

1 tablespoon oyster sauce

1 to 2 red finger-length chilies, deseeded and minced

3 tablespoons oil 4 garlic cloves, minced

Sprigs of coriander leaves (cilantro) to garnish

Marinade:

1 tablespoon fish sauce

1/3 teaspoon salt

2 teaspoons garlic, minced

Directions

In a large mixing bowl, combine all the marinade ingredients and stir thoroughly. Mix the shrimp inside the marinade until they are well covered. Allow for a minimum of 30 minutes of marinating time.

Heat oil over a high flame in a wok or big pan, then add the shrimp to stir-fry for 3 to 4 minutes, or until done. Move to a serving plate after removing from the heat.

In the same skillet, reheat all remaining oil on medium fire. Season with oyster sauce and stir-fry the garlic with chilies for 1–2 minutes, until aromatic. Remove shrimp from the wok and spoon the sauce over them. Serve immediately with steaming rice and coriander leaves (cilantro).

Nutrition: Calories 171, Fat: 2g, Net Carbs: 0.7g, Protein: 4.7g

Mandarin Fish Slices and Chrysanthemum

Preparation time: 10 minutes

Cooking Time: 55 minutes

Serving: 4

Ingredients:

1 1/2 teaspoons cornstarch

1 1/2 teaspoons Shao Hsing rice wine

1 tablespoon edible chrysanthemum petals

1 tablespoon plus 1 teaspoon egg white

1/4 cup Homemade Chicken Broth

1/4 teaspoon of white pepper, ground

12 ounces skinless sea bass fillet

2 teaspoons minced ginger

3/4 teaspoon salt

4 ounces luffa or zucchini

4 tablespoons vegetable oil

1/2 teaspoon of sesame oil

Directions

Remove any visible bones in the fish. Cut the fish in half lengthwise, following the natural deep crease of fillet, into two 2-inch broad strips. Cut 1/4-inch-thick slices along the strip on the slight diagonal, one strip at a time. Cut the slices into 2-inch-long matchsticks by stacking them. In a shallow dish, combine the fish with the egg white, 1 teaspoon of cornstarch, 1 teaspoon of rice wine, 1/4 teaspoon of salt, and pepper. To blend, gently whisk everything together. Combine 2 tablespoons of veggie oil and 1 teaspoon of cool water in a small mixing bowl.

Combine liquid broth and remaining half teaspoon of cornstarch, half teaspoon of rice wine, and 2 pinches of salt in a small mixing dish. Set aside. Peel the luffa using a vegetable peeler. When using zucchini, there is no need to peel the vegetable. Cut longitudinally in half. Cut each half into scant ¼ inch slices on the diagonal. Cut the slices into 2-inch-long matchsticks by stacking them. You'll need roughly 3/4 cup.

Over a high fire, heat a plain wok until a drop of water sputters within 1–2 seconds of touch. Add 1 tablespoon of veggie oil, 1 tablespoon of ginger. Stir-fry all fish slices in the wok for 5 seconds and spread them out evenly. Cook for 10 seconds, undisturbed. Turn the heat down right away. With a metal spatula, gently stir-fry your fish slices inside the wok until they become white and are not done through, 1–2 minutes. Place it on a platter to cool.

Stir the remaining 1 tablespoon of veggie oil into the wok on high heat for 30 seconds, and then add the luffa and the leftover 2 pinches of salt. Stir the broth mixture into the wok and bring to a boil, stirring gently for 20 to 30 seconds, or till the sauce gets thickened somewhat. Turn the heat down and add the fish. Stir-fry the ingredients for approximately 1 minute, or until the salmon is just cooked through. Drizzle the sesame oil over the top. Add the chrysanthemum petals as a finishing touch.

Nutrition: Calories 47, Fat: 0.3g, Net Carbs: 0.7g, Protein: 0.7g

Paella Seafood

Preparation time: 10 minutes

Cooking Time: 45 minutes

Serving: 4

Ingredients:

½ cup extra-virgin olive oil, divided

½ pound bay scallops

½ pound large shrimp

½ pound squid

¾ cup peas, fresh or frozen

1 pound of boneless chicken thighs, cut into bite-size pieces

1 pound mussels or clams

1 pound Spanish chorizo sausage, cut into ¼-inch slices

1 Spanish onion, diced

1 teaspoon paprika

1 teaspoon saffron threads

2 cups rice (preferably Calasparra or bomba)

4 garlic cloves, minced

4 cups shellfish or chicken broth

6 piquillo peppers, minced

Kosher salt and freshly ground black pepper

1 cup dry white wine

1 cup tomato purée

To serve:

Lemon wedges

Directions

In a wok, heat 3 tablespoons of olive oil on medium to high fire. Cook for 3 minutes on each side to brown the chicken. Sauté the onion in the leftover 5 tablespoons of olive oil until golden, approximately 5 minutes. Combine the tomato purée, peppers, garlic, and paprika in a mixing bowl. Saffron threads should be lightly crushed before being stirred into the veggies. Lightly season everything with salt and black pepper. Allow the veggies to soften for 2–3 minutes before adding the rice.

Pour the broth and wine into the pot. Stir the paella and tuck the chorizo bits in. Cook, partially covered, on medium heat for 20 to 25 minutes, stirring periodically approximately every 3–4 minutes, till the chicken with chorizo is done. Keep an eye on the rice to ensure it doesn't burn on the bottom, and reduce heat to moderate if necessary.

Cover the wok and pour the rice over the shrimp, mussels, scallops, and squid. Add the peas and mix well. Allow your paella to simmer for another 8–10 minutes, stirring regularly, in the covered wok on medium heat. Check rice for doneness at this stage; it should be almost ready. Serve along with lemon wedges after the rice and fish are fully cooked.

Nutrition: Calories 341, Fat: 11g, Net Carbs: 39g, Protein: 195

Pepper Crabs in Garlic

Preparation time: 10 minutes

Cooking Time: 20 minutes

Serving: 4

Ingredients:

½ teaspoon sugar

1 green onion (scallions), thinly sliced

1 tablespoon freshly ground black pepper

1 tablespoon garlic, minced

2 to 3 fresh medium crabs (3 pounds)

3 tablespoons oil

1/2 cup (125 milliliters) chicken stock

1/2 teaspoon salt

Directions

Thoroughly scrub and rinse the crabs. Each crab's claws should be removed. Remove carapace and throw it away. Remove any roe and toss away the gills. Rinse the crabs well before halving them with the cleaver and cracking the claws with a hammer.

Heat oil over a high flame in a wok, then stir the garlic with black pepper for 30 seconds, or until fragrant. Season the crabs with salt and sugar, then stir-fry for 2–3 minutes. Add chicken stock, stir well, and cover the wok to cook for 3–5 minutes. Finally, mix in the green onion and turn off the heat.

Immediately transfer cooked crabs to the serving plate and serve.

Nutrition: Calories 844.4, Fat: 82.3g, Net Carbs: 7g, Protein: 22.2g

Brothy Clams with Black Bean Sauce

Preparation time: 10 minutes

Cooking Time: 3 minutes

Serving: 4

ingredients

1 cup uncooked white rice

1 tablespoon cooking oil

4 garlic cloves, crushed and chopped

2 tablespoons crushed, chopped ginger

½ cup vegetable or meat broth

2 cups littleneck or mahogany clams, rinsed clean

¼ cup rice wine

2 tablespoons cornstarch

3 tablespoons black bean sauce

Directions

Prepare the rice as outlined here.

In a wok over high heat, heat the cooking oil until it shimmers.

Add the garlic and ginger and stir-fry for 1 minute.

Add the broth and bring to a boil. While waiting for the broth to boil, line a serving platter with the cooked rice.

Add the clams to the broth, cover the pan, and let steam for 2 minutes, or until the clams open.

Remove the clams and place on top of the rice, leaving the broth in the wok.

In a small bowl, whisk together the rice wine and cornstarch. Add to the broth along with the black bean sauce. Stir until a glaze forms.

Drizzle the sauce over the opened clams and rice and serve.

Nutrition: calories 140, fat 7, fiber 6, carbs 22, protein 7

Limey Vietnamese Scallops

Preparation time: 10 minutes

Cooking Time: 20 minutes

Serving: 4

Ingredients

¼ cup rice wine

¼ cup fish sauce

¼ cup brown sugar

Juice of 1 lime

1 pound (454 g) large sea scallops, cut in half widthwise

2 tablespoons cooking oil

2 garlic cloves, crushed and chopped

4 scallions, cut into 1-inch pieces

1 European cucumber, raked and cut into ¼-inch disks

1 teaspoon hot sesame oil

¼ cup rice vinegar

Directions

In a large bowl, combine the rice wine, fish sauce, brown sugar, and lime juice. Add the scallops to marinate and set aside.

In a wok over high heat, heat the cooking oil until it shimmers.

Add the garlic and scallions and stir-fry for 30 seconds.

Add the marinated scallops, reserving the marinade, and stir-fry for 30 seconds.

Add the cucumber and marinade to the wok and stir-fry for 30 seconds.

Turn off the heat and toss the cucumbers and scallops with the sesame oil and rice vinegar. Serve alone or over jasmine rice.

Nutrition: calories 140, fat 7, fiber 6, carbs 22, protein 7

Mussels with Lemongrass

Preparation time: 10 minutes

Cooking Time: 25 minutes

Serving: 4

Ingredients:

1 pound (500 grams) fresh mussels, cleaned

1 stalk lemongrass, tender inner part of bottom third only, crushed and cut into lengths

1/3 teaspoon freshly ground black pepper

1/2 cup (1/3 ounce/10 grams) Asian basil leaves

1/2 cup (125 milliliters) water 2 shallots, diced

1/2 teaspoon salt

Dipping Sauce:

1 tablespoon sugar

1 teaspoon of salt

1/3 cup (60 milliliters) fish sauce

2 garlic cloves

2 fresh coriander roots

2 or 3 red finger-length chilies

2 tablespoons fresh coriander leaves (cilantro), chopped

1/2 cup (125 milliliters) fresh lime or lemon extract

1/2 cup (125 milliliters) water

Directions

To make the Dipping Sauce, pound the garlic, chilies, and coriander roots until smooth in a pestle and mortar. Combine this paste with the other Dipping Sauce ingredients in a mixing bowl and whisk thoroughly.

Any open mussels should be discarded. Add the rest of the ingredients to the remains in a wok. Cook for 5 minutes after covering and bringing to boil on high heat. Remove the wok from heat and serve with Dipping Sauce on the side. Remove all mussels from their shells and dip them in the sauce to consume.

Nutrition: Calories 150, Fat: 5g, Net Carbs: 15g, Protein: 11g

Poached Fish With No-Cook Method

Preparation time: 10 minutes

Cooking Time: 43 minutes

Serving:

Ingredients:

1 pound meaty fish fillet, such as tuna or Mahdi, cleaned and cut into even pieces

1 scallion, julienned, both green and white parts

1 tablespoon apple cider vinegar

1 tablespoon honey

1 tablespoon soy sauce

1 teaspoon freshly ground black pepper

1 teaspoon toasted sesame oil

2 tablespoons cornstarch

2 teaspoons chili sauce

2 teaspoons sea salt

Directions

Combine the cornstarch, salt, and pepper in a mixing bowl. Dip your fish fillet over the cornstarch mixture on both sides and coat evenly. Place a fish in the wok with care.

In a separate wok, heat water to boiling. There should be sufficient water to completely submerge the fish inside the wok. When the water has reached a boil, pour this over the fish to fully cover it. Cover the wok tightly using a lid or aluminum foil. Preheat the wok and poach the salmon for 12–14 minutes.

Make the sauce by combining the soy sauce, apple cider vinegar, honey, sesame oil, and chili sauce in a mixing bowl, whereas the fish is poaching.

When fish is done, drain it and place it on a serving dish. Pour this sauce on the fish and top with the scallion juliennes.

Nutrition: Calories 343, Fat: 32g, Net Carbs: 13g, Protein: 24g

Chapter 5: Poultry Recipes

Spiced Chicken Tenders

Preparation time: 10 minutes

Cooking Time: 3 minutes

Serving: 4

Ingredients:

1 cup all-flour

1 pound chicken tenders

1 tablespoon season salt

1/2 tablespoon black pepper

1/2 tablespoon red pepper flakes

1/4 cup milk

2 cup canola oil

3 eggs

Directions

Combine the flour, seasoned salt, red pepper flakes, and black pepper in a small dish.

In a separate shallow bowl, whisk together the egg and milk. Roll all chicken tenders inside the flour mixture equally before dipping them inside the egg mixture and rolling them again in the flour mixture.

Heat oil in a big wok and cook the chicken for 5–7 minutes per side.

Place it on a platter lined with paper towels to drain the chicken.

Nutrition: Calories 248.2, Fat: 4g, Net Carbs: 22.9g, Protein: 27.7g

Spicy Cornmeal Coated Chicken

Preparation time: 10 minutes

Cooking Time: 20 minutes

Serving: 4

Ingredients:

1 teaspoon paprika

1/2 teaspoon garlic powder

1/2 teaspoon pepper

1/2 teaspoon salt

1/4 teaspoon cumin, ground

2 tablespoons cornmeal

4 medium boneless chicken halves breast, skinless

Cooking spray, non-stick

Directions

Combine all ingredients in a large mixing bowl, excluding the chicken and cooking spray. Add chicken breast halves and liberally cover them in the mixture.

Cook on medium heat in a wok greased with cooking spray.

Cook all chicken breast halves for 8–10 minutes, turning them halfway through.

Nutrition: Calories 468, Fat: 26g, Net Carbs: 17g, Protein: 38g

Party Chicken Wings

Preparation time: 10 minutes

Cooking Time: 40 minutes

Serving: 4

Ingredients:

1 teaspoon Chinese five-spice powder

1 teaspoon of salt

1/3 cup cornstarch

2 pounds chicken wings, rinsed and patted dry

2 tablespoons powdered chicken broth mix

Cooking oil for deep-frying

Directions

Divide your chicken wings into halves. Combine cornstarch, chicken broth mix, salt, and five-spice powder in a large mixing bowl. Mix in the chicken well. Allow for a 10-minute rest period.

Preheat the frying oil in a wok. Deep-fry all chicken wings in batches of a few at a time until golden brown, about 7 to 8 minutes each batch.

Nutrition: Calories 46, Fat: 3.4g, Net Carbs: 0g, Protein: 3.8g

Soy Sauce Chicken

Preparation time: 10 minutes

Cooking Time: 60 minutes

Serving: 4

Ingredients:

1 and 1/2 tablespoons sesame oil

1 whole chicken (3 to 3 half pounds)

1/2 cup dark soy sauce

1/2 cup packed brown sugar

1/2 cup rice wine

10 slices ginger, crushed

2 pieces dried tangerine peel (about 1 inch)

3 whole star anise

3/4 cup soy sauce

4 cups chicken broth

4 garlic cloves, slightly crushed

Directions

In a large wok, combine all ingredients, excluding the chicken, to make the master sauce.

Place the chicken in the wok, breast side down, on high heat; lid, and bring to boil. Reduce to a low heat setting, cover, and cook for 20 minutes. Continue to cook, covered, for a further 20 minutes after turning the chicken well in the sauce. Turn the heat down and set aside for 15 minutes, covered. Remove chicken from the pan and set it aside to cool for 20 minutes before carving.

Cut the chicken back into a chicken form and place it on a dish.

Before serving, drizzle a little of the prepared sauce over the chicken.

Nutrition: Calories 110, Fat: 3g, Net Carbs: 0g, Protein: 23g

Soy-Ginger Marinated Chicken

Preparation time: 10 minutes

Cooking Time: 65 minutes

Serving: 4

Ingredients:

1 scallion, cut into 2-inch pieces, and split in half

½-inch ginger root, crushed

1 tablespoon. sherry wine

1/2 teaspoon sugar

2 tablespoons soy sauce

1 teaspoon salt

2 1/2–3 pounds chicken, cut in 8 pieces and chop into 2-inch pieces across the bones

1/2 cup flour

3 cup peanut oil

Directions

Mix the gingerroot, scallion, wine, sugar, soy sauce, and salt in a large mixing bowl until the sugar is dissolved.

Add all chicken pieces and liberally cover them in the mixture; set aside for 1–2 hours at room temperature.

Remove your chicken pieces out from the marinade and toss them out.

Pat the chicken pieces dry with a paper towel.

Preheat oil in a wok on a medium to high flame.

Place the flour in a small dish. Using the flour, evenly coat the chicken pieces. Fry all chicken pieces for approximately 5 minutes in heated oil, flipping once or twice.

To drain the chicken, place it on paper towel-lined plates.

Nutrition: Calories 190, Fat: 8.9g, Net Carbs: 18.2g, Protein: 10.8g

Chicken with Milky Sauce

Preparation time: 10 minutes

Cooking Time: 20 minutes

Serving: 4

Ingredients:

1 cup milk

1 egg, beaten

1 cup all-flour

2 teaspoon garlic salt

1/4 teaspoon poultry seasoning

1 teaspoon paprika

1 (4 pounds) whole chicken, cut into pieces

1 cup chicken broth

1 teaspoon ground black pepper

1/2 cup milk

3 cup vegetable oil

Directions

In a small bowl, whisk together the egg and half a cup of milk. Combine the flour, garlic salt, pepper, poultry seasoning, and paprika inside a resealable plastic bag. Seal the bag after adding the chicken pieces. Toss well to cover.

Remove the chicken from the bag and place it in a shallow dish with the flour mixture.

Preheat oil in a wok. Dip the chicken into the egg mixture and coat it in the flour mixture uniformly. Preserve the rest of the flour mixture aside.

Fry all chicken pieces in heated oil until golden brown on both sides. Reduce heat to moderate and cook chicken for another 30 minutes.

Place it on a platter lined with paper towels to drain the chicken. Remove roughly 2 tablespoons of the oil from the wok and set aside.

Reduce heat to low and gradually add the remaining flour mixture, stirring constantly. Cook for approximately 2 minutes before adding the broth and stirring constantly.

Raise the temperature to high and slowly pour in the milk, stirring constantly. Bring it to a boil. Reduce to low heat and cook for approximately 5 minutes.

Pour the sauce well over the chicken right away and serve.

Nutrition: Calories 221, Fat: 7.4g, Net Carbs: 13.1g, Protein: 25.3g

Crispy Chicken

Preparation time: 10 minutes

Cooking Time: 30 minutes

Serving: 4

Ingredients:

1 cup all-flour

1 cup oil for frying, or as needed

1 egg

1/2 cup milk

1 teaspoon ground black pepper

1 teaspoon paprika

1 teaspoon salt

1/2 cup seasoned bread crumbs

2 teaspoon garlic powder

4 skinless, boneless chicken breast halves

Directions

In a small bowl, whisk together the egg and milk.

Combine the flour, garlic powder, breadcrumbs, paprika, salt, and black pepper in a separate shallow dish.

Preheat oil inside a wok. After dipping the chicken breast halves, egg mixture, evenly roll them in the flour mixture.

Cook all chicken breast halves for 10 minutes, turning halfway through.

Serve.

Nutrition: Calories 225, Fat: 10g, Net Carbs: 14.2g, Protein: 16g

Cheesy Parsley Chicken

Preparation time: 10 minutes

Cooking Time: 20 minutes

Serving: 4

Ingredients:

1 (4-pound) chicken, cut into pieces

1 crushed garlic clove

1 cup dried bread crumbs

1 teaspoon salt

1/3 cup parmesan cheese, grated

1/4 pound butter, melted

1/8 teaspoon ground black pepper

2 tablespoons parsley, diced

Directions

Before you do anything else, butter a wok.

Combine the melted butter and garlic in a shallow dish.

Combine the cheese, parsley, breadcrumbs, salt, and black pepper in a separate shallow dish.

Distribute the butter and cheese mixture evenly over the chicken pieces. Arrange all chicken pieces in a single layer in the prepared wok. Cook for approximately 1–1 1/4 hours in the wok, drizzling with the leftover butter mixture equally.

Nutrition: Calories 100, Fat: 2.5g, Net Carbs: 1g, Protein: 6g

Crispy Paprika Chicken

Preparation time: 10 minutes

Cooking Time: 20 minutes

Serving: 4

Ingredients:

1 (4 pounds) chicken, cut into pieces

1 cup buttermilk

1 teaspoon paprika

2 cups all-flour for coating

2 quarts of veggie oil for frying

Salt and pepper to taste

Directions

Place the buttermilk in a small bowl.

Place the salt, flour, black pepper, and paprika in a separate shallow dish. Completely cover all chicken pieces in buttermilk before coating them inside the flour mixture.

Place the chicken pieces in a wok, cover with wax paper, and set aside until the flour is pasty.

Heat your veggie-oiling big wok and brown the chicken pieces.

Reduce heat to low and cook for approximately 30 minutes, covered. Cook until crispy, then uncover and raise the heat.

Place it on a platter lined with paper towels to drain the chicken.

Nutrition: Calories 280, Fat: 7.1g, Net Carbs: 30g, Protein: 23.9g

Chicken Steaks with Gravy

Preparation time: 10 minutes

Cooking Time: 40 minutes

Serving: 4

Ingredients:

4 (1/2 pound) chicken cube steaks

1/4 cup+ 2 cup all-flour

1 teaspoon baking soda

2 teaspoons baking powder

1 teaspoon black pepper

1 and 1/2 cup buttermilk

1 egg

1 tablespoon hot pepper sauce

2 garlic cloves, minced

3 cup vegetable shortening for deep frying

3/4 teaspoon salt

4 cup milk

Kosher salt and ground black pepper to taste

Directions

Pound the steaks into 1/4-inch thickness using a meat pounder.

Combine the flour, salt, baking soda, baking powder, and black pepper in a small dish.

Whisk the egg, buttermilk, spicy sauce, and garlic in a separate shallow dish.

Coat the steaks in flour, and then dip them inside the egg mixture before coating them again in flour.

Preheat oil in a big wok. Fry the steaks for 3–5 minutes on all sides after adding them to the wok.

To drain the steaks, place them on paper towel-lined platters. Drain the grease from the wok, leaving 1/4 cup of mixture in the wok.

Slowly add remaining flour, constantly stirring in a medium-low heat wok.

Slowly pour in the milk, stirring constantly, and turn the heat to medium.

Cook for around 6–7 minutes at a low temperature. Remove from the fire after adding the salt and pepper.

Serve the chicken with the gravy on top.

Nutrition: Calories 245, Fat: 9g, Net Carbs: 8g, Protein: 31g

Crispy Pheasant

Preparation time: 10 minutes

Cooking Time: 30 minutes

Serving: 4

Ingredients:

1 and a half tablespoon white vinegar, distilled

1 cup canola oil for frying

1 cup of saltine cracker crumbs, finely crushed

1 cup milk

2 pheasant breast halves, thinly sliced

Directions

Combine the vinegar and milk in a small bowl.

Place your cracker crumbs in a separate shallow dish.

After dipping pheasant slices inside the vinegar mixture, equally, coat them with the crumbs.

Cook all pheasant slices for approximately 5 minutes per side in a large wok on medium to high heat.

To drain pheasant slices, place them on paper towel-lined plates.

Nutrition: Calories 335, Fat: 17g, Net Carbs: 0g, Protein: 45g

Crispy Chicken Croquettes

Preparation time: 10 minutes

Cooking Time: 60 minutes

Serving: 4

Ingredients:

1/4 cup butter

1/4 cup flour

1/2 cup chicken broth

1/2 cup milk

2 eggs, beaten

3 cup finely chopped cooked chicken

1 and 1/2 cup seasoned bread crumbs, divided

1 tablespoon dried parsley

1/4 cup minced onion

1/8 teaspoon celery seed

1/4 teaspoon garlic powder

1/4 cup oil, or as needed

1/8 teaspoon cayenne pepper

Salt and ground black pepper to taste

Directions

Melt the butter in a wok on medium heat. Cook for approximately 1 minute, constantly stirring as you add the flour. Slowly pour in the broth and milk, pounding constantly. Cook for 5–10 minutes, constantly stirring until a thick sauce develops. Remove wok from heat and set it aside to cool for approximately 10 minutes. Combine the cooled sauce, eggs, chicken, 1 cup of breadcrumbs, parsley, onion, celery seeds, cayenne pepper, garlic powder, salt, and black pepper in a large mixing bowl and mix thoroughly. Cover and marinate for approximately 2 hours in the refrigerator.

From the ingredients, make 6 equal-sized patties.

Place the leftover breadcrumbs in a shallow dish. Roll the breadcrumbs around each burger.

Heat oil in a big wok on medium heat and cook all patties for approximately 5 minutes per side.

To drain the chicken, place it on a paper towel-lined plate.

Nutrition: Calories 208.3, Fat: 8.5g, Net Carbs: 14.5g, Protein: 18.6g

Chapter 6: Beef, pork and lamb Recipes

Vegetable Lo Mein

Preparation time: 10 minutes

Cooking Time: 25 minutes

Serving: 4

Ingredients:

2 tablespoons of soy sauce

2 teaspoons sugar

1 teaspoon of sesame oil

1 teaspoon chili sauce (optional)

1 tablespoon peanut oil

2 garlic cloves, minced

1½ cups cremini or button mushrooms, sliced

1 red bell pepper, julienned

¼ cup shredded carrots

½ cup snow peas

2 scallions, cut into one-inch pieces

½ pound lo Mein, cooked according to package directions and drained well

Directions

Combine the sugar, soy sauce, sesame oil, and chili sauce in a mixing bowl to make the sauce. Set aside.

Heat the wok on high until a droplet of water sizzles when it comes into contact with it. Add in the peanut oil to cover your wok. Stir-fry the cremini mushrooms, garlic, red bell pepper, and carrots for 3–4 minutes, stirring often.

Stir in the snow peas and scallions for a further 2–3 minutes. In a wok, combine all Lo Mein and sauce mixture. Take off the heat and toss together everything to mix. Serve right away.

Nutrition: Calories 184, Fat: 8.39g, Net Carbs: 12.3g, Protein: 14.3g

Beef Chow Fun

Preparation time: 10 minutes

Cooking Time: 30 minutes

Serving: 4

Ingredients:

2 tablespoons dark soy sauce, divided

2 teaspoons Shaoxing rice wine or dry sherry

1 teaspoon of cornstarch

½ pound flank steak, cut into strips across the grain

1 tablespoon light soy sauce

⅓ cup beef or vegetable broth

1 tablespoon oyster sauce

2 tablespoons peanut or vegetable oil

1 sweet onion, thinly sliced

3 scallions, cut into one-inch pieces

½ pound dried wide chow fun rice noodles, soaked according to package directions and drained well

Directions

Combine 1 tablespoon of dark soy sauce, rice wine, and cornstarch in a medium mixing bowl. Toss the steak in the basin to evenly coat it on both sides. Allow 10 minutes for the steak to marinate.

Combine the remaining 1 tablespoon of dark soy sauce, beef broth, light soy sauce, and oyster sauce in a small dish to make the sauce. Set aside.

Preheat your wok to medium-high. Add in the peanut oil to cover your wok. Stir in the onion and cook for approximately 1 minute. Stir-fry the steak with the scallions in the wok for approximately 1 minute, or till the meat is done. Toss in the noodles and whisk to incorporate everything.

Stir and toss the sauce mixture into the wok to incorporate. Cook for another 2 minutes.

Nutrition: Calories 192, Fat: 7g, Net Carbs: 20g, Protein: 10g

Dan Noodles

Preparation time: 10 minutes

Cooking Time: 25 minutes

Serving: 4

Ingredients:

2 tablespoons peanut or vegetable oil

12 ounces ground pork

Sea salt

Freshly ground black pepper

2 tablespoons fresh chopped, peeled ginger

¾ cup chicken broth

2 tablespoons chili oil

1 tablespoon rice vinegar

2 tablespoons of soy sauce

½ teaspoon of sesame oil

2 tablespoons peanut butter

1 teaspoon Sichuan peppercorns

½ pound dried egg noodles, cooked according to package directions, well-drained

2 tablespoons chopped, roasted peanuts

3 scallions, thinly sliced

Directions

Preheat your wok to medium-high heat. Add in the peanut oil to cover the wok. Stir-fry the pork for approximately 2 minutes, seasoning it with sea salt and pepper. Stir in the ginger and cook for approximately 2 minutes with the meat.

Combine the chicken broth, rice vinegar, chili oil, soy sauce, peanut butter, sesame oil, and Sichuan peppercorns in a large mixing bowl. Toss everything together and cook for 6–8 minutes, or till sauce thickens. Remove your wok from heat and turn it off. Toss the peanuts, noodles, and scallions together in the wok to incorporate everything. Serve right away.

Beef Tri-Tip

Preparation time: 10 minutes

Cooking Time: 65minutes

Serving: 4

Ingredients:

1 and 1/2 cups red wine

1/4 cup minced ginger

1/4 cup soy sauce

2 pounds beef tri-tip

2 tablespoons dark soy sauce

2 tablespoons sugar

3 tablespoons garlic, minced

1/2 head small iceberg lettuce, julienned

1 cup chopped cilantro

Directions

Place the meat in a plastic bag that can be resealable. Combine the soy sauce, wine, sugar, dark soy sauce, ginger, cilantro, and garlic in a bowl to make the marinade. Seal the bag after pouring the marinade on the meat. Refrigerate for 4 hours, preferably overnight, shaking the bag now and then.

Remove the meat from the marinade and set this on a rack inside a foil-lined wok 6 inches from the broiler. On each side, broil your tri-tip for 8–10 minutes. Remove the tri-tip from the oven and set it aside for 20 minutes before cutting.

Serve it on a lettuce bed.

Nutrition: Calories 200, Fat: 11g, Net Carbs: 0g, Protein: 23g

Egg Fried Rice

Preparation time: 10 minutes

Cooking Time: 22 minutes

Serving: 4

Ingredients:

4 tablespoons peanut oil, divided

2 tablespoons garlic, minced

2 tablespoons grated fresh ginger

1 small sweet onion, diced

4 cups cooked long-grain or jasmine rice (day-old rice is best)

4 large eggs, beaten

2 teaspoons of sesame oil

4 teaspoons soy sauce

Sea salt

Freshly ground pepper

Directions

Preheat your wok to medium-high. Add in 3 tablespoons of peanut oil to cover your wok. Stir in the ginger and garlic for 1 minute.

Stir in the onion and cook for approximately 3 minutes, till it is soft. Turn the heat down to medium. Toss in the rice and mix everything in the wok. Stir-frying should be continued for another 2 minutes.

Move your rice to the wok's outer borders. Pour all eggs into the middle of the wok, if required, before adding the remainder 1 tablespoon of peanut oil. Cook for 1 minute to scramble the eggs

Turn off the heat once the eggs are scrambled. Combine the eggs and rice in a mixing bowl. Combine the rice, sesame oil, and soy sauce in a large mixing bowl. Season with pepper and salt to taste.

Nutrition: Calories 209, Fat: 5.6g, Net Carbs: 32.1g, Protein: 4.3g

Fried Pineapple Rice

Preparation time: 10 minutes

Cooking Time: 35 minutes

Serving: 4

Ingredients:

3 tablespoons soy sauce

1 tablespoon sesame oil

2 tablespoons peanut oil

2 garlic cloves, minced

1 sweet onion, diced

1 large carrot, julienned

½ cup sweet corn

½ cup peas, fresh or frozen

3 cups cooked long-grain rice (day-old rice is best)

2 cups pineapple, drained (fresh or canned)

½ cup ham or Canadian bacon

2 scallions, thinly sliced

¼ cup cashews halved lengthwise

Sea salt

Freshly ground black pepper

Directions

Combine the soy sauce and sesame oil in a small bowl. Set aside.

Heat the wok on a high flame till a droplet of water sputters when it comes into contact with it. Add in the peanut oil to cover your wok. Stir-fry for around 2 minutes with the garlic and onion. Stir-fry the carrots, corn, and peas in the wok for 3 to 4 minutes, or until crisp-tender.

Reduce heat to medium and add the rice, ham, pineapple, and scallions to the pan. Combine the soy sauce and water in a mixing bowl. Continue to stir and cook for another 3 to 4 minutes till everything is thoroughly mixed. Season with pepper and salt after adding the cashews.

Nutrition: Calories 1448, Fat: 48.1g, Net Carbs: 216g, Protein: 28.3g

Grilled Rib-Eye in Flavored Butter

Preparation time: 10 minutes

Cooking Time: 25 minutes

Serving: 4

Ingredients:

1 2½–to 3-inch-thick bone-in rib-eye steak (2½–3 pounds)

1 teaspoon freshly ground black pepper

1½ teaspoons salt

2 teaspoons extra-virgin olive oil

Flavored butter

Directions

Rub the meat on both sides with the oil. Season liberally with 3/4 teaspoon of salt and half teaspoon of pepper on each side. Place your steak on a dish and set it aside to rest for 2 hours at room temperature. The interior temperature should be between 50 and 60 degrees Fahrenheit.

For indirect grilling, use a charcoal or gas wok.

Brush the grill with a light coating of oil. Grill the steak for 2–3 minutes, or until deep brown, directly on hot coals or fire. If flare-ups occur, transfer the steak to an area of the grill where there is no fire, then wait for flare-ups to decrease before returning it to heat and searing it. Turn and sear the opposite side for 2–3 minutes, or until a rich brown color has developed but not burnt.

Move the steak to the grill portion with no fire, with bone facing the heat, to prevent the meat from burning. Cook for 10 to 15 minutes on the grill, or till the internal temperature rises 120°F to 125°F as rare, 125°F–130°F for very rare, or 130°F–135°F for moderate. Transfer your steak to a heated serving plate and cover loosely with aluminum foil to rest for 10 minutes. Place three 14-inch-thick pats of seasoned butter just on meat after 5 minutes. Its temperature will climb by 10 to 15 degrees as the steak sits.

Remove the meat from the bone and cut it into 12-inch-thick slices crosswise. Serve immediately with melted butter spooned over the pieces.

Nutrition: Calories 302.5, Fat: 16.5g, Net Carbs: 1.1g, Protein: 34.8g

Indonesian Fried Rice (Nasi Goreng)

Preparation time: 10 minutes

Cooking Time: 40 minutes

Serving: 4

Nutrition: Calories 706, Fat: 18g, Net Carbs: 107g, Protein: 29g

Ingredients:

2 tablespoons peanut or vegetable oil

3 garlic cloves, minced

2 teaspoons fresh ginger, grated

1 cup of beef, chicken, or shrimp, thinly sliced (if desired)

2 tablespoons of soy sauce

1 tablespoon kecap manis

1 teaspoon of sesame oil

4 cups cooked long-grain or jasmine rice (day-old rice is best)

4 eggs, fried sunny-side up

Sambal oelek, for garnish

Directions

Heat the wok on a high flame till a droplet of water sputters when it comes into contact with it. Add in the peanut oil to cover your wok. Stir-fry the ginger and garlic for around 20 seconds. Stir-fry until 2 minutes with the meat.

Reduce to low heat and stir in the soy sauce, sesame oil, kecap Manis, and rice. To combine the components, mix and whisk them together. Stir-fry for 2–3 minutes more.

Serve with the fried egg atop and sambal oelek just on the side in four servings.

Nutrition: Calories 329, Fat: 8g, Net Carbs: 55g, Protein: 13g

Seared Rib Eyes with Easy Herb Butter

Preparation time: 10 minutes

Cooking Time: 55 minutes

Serving: 4

Ingredients:

For the herb butter:

½ cup (1 stick) unsalted butter, softened

1 tablespoon fresh chives, finely chopped

1 teaspoon chopped fresh thyme

2 tablespoons grated parmesan

For the steaks:

2 tablespoons vegetable oil

3 cloves of garlic, crushed but still whole

Kosher salt and freshly ground black pepper

2 1½-inch-thick rib-eye steaks, 1 pound almost each

Directions

Remove the steaks from the refrigerator an hour when you're about to cook and allow them to reach room temperature.

Mix the chives, butter, thyme, and Parmesan in a small bowl to prepare the herb butter. Roll the butter into a cylinder using your hands after covering it in plastic wrap. Refrigerate the butter for at least 30 minutes to stiffen it up.

Heat oil plus garlic inside a wok on high fire to make the steaks. Allow 2 minutes for the garlic to color and absorb the oil before discarding it.

Using salt and pepper, season the steaks. For medium-rare, cook all steaks in the garlic-infused oil for approximately 5 minutes per side. Allow them ample interaction time with a wok to generate a good sear by not moving them about too much.

Serve the steaks with 1–2 teaspoons of herb butter on the side. As quickly as the butter has melted, serve.

Nutrition: Calories 241, Fat: 16g, Net Carbs: 1g, Protein: 235

Shirataki Stir-Fry

Preparation time: 10 minutes

Cooking Time: 28 minutes

Serving: 4

Ingredients:

1 pound Shirataki noodles

¼ cup soy sauce

2 teaspoons hoisin sauce

1 tablespoon cornstarch

½ cup warm or room temperature water

1 tablespoon peanut oil

2 cups broccoli florets

½ pound boneless, skinless chicken breast, cut into thin strips

1 cup bean sprouts, washed and dried well

½ cup chopped cremini mushrooms

½ cup thinly sliced zucchini

¼ cup shredded carrots

2 scallions, chopped

Directions

Under cold running water, thoroughly rinse the Shirataki noodles. After thoroughly draining them, cut them into little pieces twice using culinary shears. Set aside.

Combine the soy sauce, cornstarch, hoisin sauce, and water in a small bowl to form a sauce. Set aside.

Preheat your wok to medium-high. Add in the oil to cover your wok. Stir in the broccoli and chicken for 5–6 minutes, or till the chicken is done through. Stir-fry for 2–3 minutes with bean sprouts, zucchini, mushrooms, carrots, and scallions.

Pour all sauce into wok, toss to incorporate with the chicken and broccoli, and simmer for approximately 2 minutes, or until the sauce thickens. Add cooked noodles to the pan, toss with other ingredients, then cook for 2–3 minutes, tossing regularly, until the flavors are well mixed.

Nutrition: Calories 258, Fat: 7.6g, Net Carbs: 16g, Protein: 30g

Singaporean Rice Noodles

Preparation time: 10 minutes

Cooking Time: 35 minutes

Serving: 4

Ingredients:

½ cup chicken broth

¼ cup soy sauce

2 tablespoons Shaoxing rice wine

2 teaspoons garlic, minced

½ teaspoon ground ginger

1 teaspoon sambal oelek

1 tablespoon peanut oil

2 bell peppers, 1 red, and 1 green, if possible, thinly sliced

2 shallots, thinly sliced

1½ cups bean sprouts

1 teaspoon curry powder

1 cup sliced mushrooms, preferably shiitake

6 ounces thin rice noodles, soaked according to package directions, drained well

1 scallion, sliced (optional garnish)

Directions

Combine chicken broth, soy sauce, garlic, rice wine, ginger, and sambal oelek in a medium bowl to make the sauce. Set aside.

Heat the wok on a high flame till a droplet of water sputters when it comes into contact with it. Add in the oil to cover your wok. Stir-fry for 2–3 minutes with the bell peppers, bean sprouts, shallots, and curry powder. Stir in the mushrooms for 2 minutes more, or when the peppers become crisp-tender.

Reduce heat to medium and toss in the noodles with 3 tablespoons of the sauce in the pan. Stir-fry and mix for 2 minutes, or until the noodles and sauce are well blended with the other ingredients.

Turn the heat down and carefully pour in the leftover sauce, constantly stirring to ensure that everything is well combined. If you prefer less sauce, don't use all of it.

Serve the noodles with sliced scallion on top.

Nutrition: Calories 193, Fat: 6.2g, Net Carbs: 30g, Protein: 3.2g

Chapter 7: Rice and Noodles Recipes

Rice with Bok Choy

Preparation time: 5 minutes

Cooking time: 30 minutes

Servings: 4

Ingredients:

1 tablespoon butter 1 head of bok choy, chopped

2 cups of chicken broth

1 cup uncooked jasmine rice

1 tablespoon of olive oil

1 tablespoon of chopped fresh chives, or to taste

1 pinch of ground black pepper

Preparation:

Melt the butter in a deep wok or large saucepan over medium heat. Add the bok choy and stir-fry for approx. 5 minutes until soft.

Add the chicken stock and turn up the heat on high. Bring to a boil. Add rice, olive oil and chives and stir well.

Cover with a tightly fitting lid, reduce the heat to a boiling point and cook for 20 minutes. After 10 minutes, check the rice to make sure it is pacing well; Overcooking makes the rice dry, undercooking results in hard rice.

Season with pepper and serve.

Nutrition: Calories: 278; Fat: 2.9g; Carbs: 59g; Protein: 6.6g

Fried rice with corned beef, spinach and eggs

Preparation time: 10 minutes

Cooking time: 15 minutes

Servings: 8

Ingredients:

1 tablespoon of vegetable oil

2 cups of shredded and chopped cooked corned beef

110 g spinach, chopped

3 eggs, lightly beaten

5 cups of cooked rice

1 teaspoon garlic powder, or according to taste

Salt to taste

Preparation:

Heat vegetable oil in a large pan or wok over medium heat. Fry and stir the corned beef for 3 minutes until completely heated; add the spinach.

Cook the spinach for 2 minutes and stir until it has wilted.

Place the spinach and beef on one side of the pan; Put eggs in the middle. Cook for 3 minutes, stirring regularly, until the eggs are whiskey.

stir in rice; Cook for 5 minutes until it is completely heated. Sprinkle with salt and garlic powder to season.

Nutrition: calories 368, fat 5.1, fiber 0.5, carbs 1.3, protein 4.6

Asian shrimp rice bowl

Preparation time: 15 minutes

Cooking time: 1 hour 30 minutes

Servings: 4

Ingredients:

1/3 cup soy sauce

1/4 cup hoisin sauce

2 tablespoons of honey

1 tablespoon of chilies paste

2 tablespoons of orange jam

225 g cooked prawns

2 cups uncooked jasmine rice

3 cups of water

2 tablespoons. olive oil

1 orange pepper, cut into cubes

1 red pepper, cut into cubes

2 cups of sugar snap peas

1 sweet onion, cut into cubes

4 cloves of garlic, chopped

2 teaspoons of chopped fresh ginger root

1/4 teaspoon sesame oil

1 1/2 teaspoons of sesame seeds

Preparation:

Mix the honey, orange jam, hoisin sauce, soy sauce and chili paste in a small bowl. Mix the prawns into the marinade and store in the refrigerator for 1 hour.

Boil a saucepan with water and rice over high heat. Reduce the heat to medium-low, then cover the saucepan and simmer for 20-25 minutes, until the rice is soft and the water has been absorbed by the rice.

Heat a large pan or wok with oil. Cook red peppers, sugar snap peas, onions and orange peppers in hot oil for 2-3 minutes and stir until the vegetables soften.

Mix in the ginger, garlic, sesame oil and the marinated prawns. Cook the whole thing for another 2-3 minutes and stir until the prawns are fully heated.

Serve this dish with hot jasmine rice and a dash of sesame seeds.

Nutrition: Calories: 321 Fat: 8g Carbohydrates: 5g Protein: 4g

Breakfast of fried brown rice

Preparation time: 5 minutes

Cooking time: 10 minutes

Servings: 4

Ingredients:

3 tablespoons of peanut oil, split or more as needed

1/2 onion, chopped

2 large eggs

1 cup of diced, fully cooked ham

2 tablespoons of butter

3 cups of cooked brown rice

kosher salt and freshly ground black pepper to taste

1/2 cup of grated cheddar cheese

Preparation:

Preheat a pan or wok on high heat for 1 minute.

Add 2 tablespoons of peanut oil to the wok, rock the wok to distribute the oil evenly on the hob and turn the heat to medium. Saute the onions for 3 minutes or until the onions start to soften.

Stir the eggs quickly for about 1 1/2 minutes, until the eggs are stirred and just start to set, but still contain a little egg liquid.

Put in the ham and stir-fry it for about 1 minute until it is almost warmed up. Add the remaining 1 tablespoon of peanut oil and butter to the same wok and let it warm up for 10 seconds.

Add the rice and cook for 3-4 minutes, stirring constantly, then add more oil if necessary to prevent the rice from sticking.

Season to taste with pepper and salt and finally sprinkle some cheddar cheese on top.

Nutrition: Calories: 191 Total Fat: 10g Saturated Fat: 3g Cholesterol: 15mg Carbohydrates: 14g Fiber: 14g Protein: 12g Phosphorus: 189mg Potassium: 327mg Sodium: 40mg

Fried rice with chicken, sugar snap peas and cashew nuts

Preparation time: 15 minutes

Cooking time: 15 minutes

Servings: 4

Ingredients:

450 g skinless and boned chicken breast, cut into thin strips

1/4 cup teriyaki sauce, divided

3 tablespoons of vegetable oil, divided

3 spring onions, thinly sliced

2 cloves of garlic, chopped

1 tablespoon of chopped fresh ginger root

8 ounces of sweet peas, sliced

1/4 cup low-sodium chicken stock

4 cups of cooked white rice

3 tablespoons of chopped roasted cashew nuts

Directions

Mix 2 tablespoons of teriyaki sauce with the chicken in a bowl. Heat a large pan or wok with 1 1/2 tablespoons of vegetable oil over high heat. Add the marinated chicken and stir-fry for 3-5 minutes or until it is no longer pink on the inside.

Stir the ginger, spring onions, remaining vegetable oil and garlic in the same wok and sauté for about 1 minute until fragrant. Stir in the chicken broth and sugar snap peas, cover the wok and cook the mixture for 2-3 minutes until tender.

Add the cooked chicken, remaining teriyaki sauce and rice to the wok and stir-fry for 2-3 minutes until the rice is cooked through.

Finally sprinkle the cashew nuts on top.

Nutrition: Calories: 191 Total Fat: 10g Saturated Fat: 3g Cholesterol: 15mg Carbohydrates: 14g Fiber: 14g Protein: 12g Phosphorus: 189mg Potassium: 327mg Sodium: 40mg

Fried rice with duck

Preparation time: 15 minutes

Cooking time: 35 minutes

Servings: 4

Ingredients:

1 cup minced Chinese roast duck, skin and fat removed and set aside

1/2 cup thinly sliced Chinese grilled pork

6 green onions, thinly sliced

2 tablespoons of soy sauce

2 eggs, beaten

3 cups of cooked long grain rice

Salt and pepper to taste

Directions

Heat a large pan or wok on medium heat and add the duck skin and fat. Fry the duck skin and fat for about 10 minutes until the fat has melted and the duck skin is crispy.

Raise the temperature to medium to high heat, then add the duck and pork. Also add about half of the green onions and the soy sauce. Keep cooking and stirring until the meat is cooked through.

This should take about 5 minutes - Add rice. Add the rice and stir for 5 minutes until the rice sizzles and is hot. Divide the rice in half and make a wide indentation in the rice so that the bottom of the wok is exposed. Pour in the beaten eggs and quickly start mixing them. From here you can then start to stir the scrambled eggs into the rice. Don't forget to add the remaining green onions!

Continue stirring for 5 minutes or until the rice is very hot. Season with salt and pepper and serve.

Nutrition: calories 368, fat 5.1, fiber 0.5, carbs 1.3, protein 4.6

Fried rice with lychee

Preparation time: 15 minutes

Cooking time: 1 hour 30 minutes

Servings: 4

Ingredients:

1 cup uncooked jasmine rice

1/2 cup of water

3 tablespoons of vegetable oil

2 cloves of garlic, chopped

2 tablespoons of chopped carrots

1 tablespoon of chopped onion

3 tablespoons. Soy-based liquid seasoning

1/4 cup reduced sodium soy sauce

2 tbsp chopped green onion

1 tbsp chopped cashew nuts

1 teaspoon raisins

1/4 teaspoon white sugar

1/4 teaspoon white pepper

5 drained and quartered lychees from the tin

Directions

Put water and rice in a saucepan and bring to a boil over high heat. Cover the saucepan, then reduce the heat to medium-low and simmer for 20-25 minutes, until the rice is soft and the rice has soaked up the water.

Put the cooked rice in a shallow bowl and store it in the refrigerator until it has cooled down. Alternatively, you can use 1 1/2 cups of leftover cooked rice.

Heat a large pan or wok with oil over medium to high heat. Add the garlic and sauté for a few seconds until it is fragrant. Add the onion and carrots and continue to fry the mixture until the onions start to soften.

Add the cold rice and stir-fry until it is hot.

Mix in the soy spice, soy sauce, white pepper, salt, spring onions, raisins and cashew nuts.

Sear the rice mixture while stirring and add the quartered lychees. Serve.

Nutrition: calories 368, fat 5.1, fiber 0.5, carbs 1.3, protein 4.6

Garlicky Shrimp Mei Fun

Preparation time: 10 minutes

Cooking Time: 25 minutes

Serving: 4

Ingredients

1 tablespoon Shaoxing wine

1 teaspoon sugar

1 tablespoon soy sauce

1 tablespoon oyster sauce

1 teaspoon sesame oil

2 tablespoons peanut or vegetable oil

1 onion, thinly sliced

1 garlic clove, minced

1 red bell pepper, sliced into strips

1 cup shrimp, pork, chicken, beef, or tofu, thinly sliced

2 eggs, beaten

10 ounces (283 g) rice noodles, soaked, drained well

1 scallion, cut into slivers

Directions

In a small bowl, make the sauce by combining the rice wine, sugar, soy sauce, oyster sauce, and sesame oil. Set aside.

Heat your wok on high until a drop of water sizzles on contact. Add the peanut oil and swirl to coat the wok. Add the onion, garlic, and red bell pepper, and stir-fry for about 20 seconds. Add the shrimp and stir-fry for 1 to 2 minutes. Slowly stream in the eggs to create egg threads, and stir-fry for about 1 minute more. Add the rice noodles and stir-fry for about 2 minutes, tossing everything together.

Add the sauce mixture to the wok. Stir-fry for 1 to 2 minutes, making sure everything is combined. Add the slivered scallion, give it a quick toss, and turn off the heat.

Serve with rice and chili sauce or sambal oelek on the side.

Nutrition: Calories 165, Fat: 5g, Net Carbs: 3g, Protein: 28g

Koa Pad Lin Gee

Preparation time: 15 minutes

Cooking time: 30 minutes

Servings: 4

Ingredients:

1 cup uncooked jasmine rice

1/2 cup of water

3 tablespoons of vegetable oil

2 cloves of garlic, chopped

2 tablespoons of chopped carrot

1 tablespoon of chopped onion

3 tablespoons of liquid soy-based seasoning

1/4 cup soy sauce with reduced sodium content

2 tablespoons of chopped green onion

1 tablespoon of chopped cashew nuts

1 teaspoon raisins

1/4 teaspoon white sugar

1/4 teaspoon white pepper

5 canned lychees, drained and quartered

Directions

Bring rice and water to a boil in a saucepan over high heat. Reduce the heat to medium to low, cover and simmer for 20 to 25 minutes, until the rice is soft and the liquid has been absorbed.

After cooking, place the rice in a shallow bowl and place in the refrigerator until cold, or use 1 1/2 cups of remaining cooked rice.

Stir in the garlic and cook for a few seconds until it smells fragrant, then stir in the carrots and onion and keep cooking until the onion starts to soften.

Add the cold rice, cook and stir until it is hot. Add the soy sauce, soy seasoning, green onions, cashew nuts, raisins, salt and white pepper.

Cook and stir until hot, then stir in the quartered lychees and serve.

Nutrition: Calories: 191 Total Fat: 10g Saturated Fat: 3g Cholesterol: 15mg Carbohydrates: 14g Fiber: 14g Protein: 12g Phosphorus: 189mg Potassium: 327mg Sodium: 40mg

Mushroom and Chicken Noodle Soup

Preparation time: 10 minutes

Cooking Time: 11 minutes

Serving: 4

Ingredients

2 teaspoons vegetable oil

2 tablespoons minced garlic

⅓ cup fresh ginger, finely chopped, peeled

5 ounces (142 g) fresh shiitake mushrooms, stemmed and thinly sliced

½ cup Shaoxing wine or good dry sherry

6 cups low-sodium chicken broth

1½ pounds (680 g) boneless chicken thighs, fat trimmed, cut into bite-size pieces

5 scallions, green part only, cut into 1-inch pieces

3 carrots, cut into matchsticks

2 tablespoons soy sauce

Sea salt

Freshly ground black pepper

Directions

½ pound (227 g) rice stick noodles, soaked in boiling water for 10 minutes and then drained

Heat your wok to medium-high heat, and then add the oil. Add the garlic, ginger, and shiitake mushrooms to the wok, and stir-fry for about 1 minute. Stir in the rice wine, reduce the heat to medium, and cook for 2 to 3 minutes. Add the chicken broth to the wok, and bring it to a hard simmer.

Add the chicken, scallions, and carrots to the soup, stir, and let it simmer for about 3 minutes. Then reduce the heat to low, and simmer for another 5 to 6 minutes. Add the soy sauce to the soup, stir to combine, and then season with the sea salt and pepper.

Divide the noodles among 4 soup bowls. Ladle the soup over the noodles and serve.

Nutrition: Calories: 355 Fat: 21g Carbohydrates: 3g Protein: 37g

Peanuts and Noodle Soup

Preparation time: 5 minutes

Cooking time: 5 minutes

Servings: 1

Ingredients:

Chili paste, to taste

1¼ cups chicken stock

2 teaspoons soy sauce

½ cup stir-fry vegetables

1 sheet straight-to-wok noodle

Crushed peanuts

Directions

In a wok, boil the stock, then add 1 sheet of straight-to-wok noodles, along with a squeeze of chili paste and soy sauce.

Continue cooking for a few minutes or until all of the noodles have separated.

Toss in a handful of stir-fry vegetables, reserving any green bits for later.

Cook for 1 minute, or until the vegetables are just soft.

Add the leafy greens and cook for another minute.

Serving Suggestions: Serve in a deep bowl, scattered with crushed peanuts.

Variation Tip: You can also use coconut aminos instead of soy sauce.

Nutrition

Calories: 274 | Fat: 12.5g | Sat Fat: 1.8g | Carbohydrates: 5.7g | Fiber: 0.7g | Sugar: 2.3g | Protein: 35.6g

Pork Fried Rice

Preparation time: 15 minutes

Cooking time: 20 minutes

Servings: 4

Ingredients:

400 g pork fillets

1/3 cup vegetable oil

4 free range eggs, lightly beaten

1 small red onion, finely diced

1 tablespoon of finely diced ginger

2 teaspoons of white sugar

2 tablespoons of hoisin sauce

2 tablespoons of light soy sauce

1 tablespoon of malt vinegar

1/4 teaspoon sesame oil

4 cups of steamed rice

2/3 cup finely chopped green onions

Directions

Cut the pork tenderloin into 5 mm slices with a sharp knife, then cut into 5 mm strips and set aside. Heat half of the oil in a hot wok until the surface appears to be slightly shimmering.

Put the beaten eggs in the wok and cook for 10 seconds on the bottom of the wok before placing the egg mixture on itself with a spatula and gently stirring for about 1 minute or until it is almost cooked.

Carefully remove the omelette from the wok with a spatula and drain on kitchen paper. Heat the remaining oil in a hot wok and stir-fry the onion and ginger for 30 seconds. Add sugar and stir-fry for 30 seconds. Add the pork and stir-fry for another 30 seconds.

Stir in hoisin sauce, soy sauce, vinegar and sesame oil and cook for 1 minute while stirring. Add rice and the reserved omelette and stir-fry for 1 minute, breaking the egg into smaller pieces with a spatula.

Finally add the spring onions and fry for another 30 seconds, stirring, until the rice is well mixed and heated through.

Nutrition: Calories: 321 Fat: 8g Carbohydrates: 5g Protein: 4g

Rice fried with bacon

Preparation time: 5 minutes

Cooking time: 30 minutes

Servings: 4

Ingredients:

225 g bacon, cut into small pieces

2 tablespoons of soy sauce

2 green onions, chopped

1/4 teaspoon sea salt

2 cups of steamed white rice

Directions

Put the bacon in a wok or a large pan and cook over medium heat for about 5 minutes, stirring occasionally, until it starts to brown.

Pour the soy sauce on top and scrape up the brown pieces from the bottom of the wok. Add green onions and salt; Cook for 30 seconds to 1 minute until wilted. add rice; Cook for 3 to 4 minutes, stirring frequently, until the soy sauce is heated through.

Nutrition: Calories: 349 Fat: 1.9g Carbohydrates: 7g Protein: 3g

Chapter 8: Soups and sauces Recipes

Hot-Sour Seafood and Vegetables Soup

Preparation time: 10 minutes

Cooking Time: 8 minutes

Serving: 4

Ingredients:

¼ pound (113 g) medium shrimp, shelled and deveined

¼ pound (113 g) sea scallops, cut in half widthwise

¼ pound (113 g) white fish (like cod or haddock), cut into 1-inch pieces

¼ pound (113 g) ground pork

1 cup chopped bok choy

4 scallions, cut into ½-inch pieces

½ cup julienned carrots

3 quarts vegetable, fish, or meat broth

¼ cup rice vinegar

2 garlic cloves, crushed and chopped

2 tbsps. Cornstarch

1 tbsp. Cooking oil

1 tbsp. Hot sesame oil

1 tbsp. Ginger, crushed and chopped

Directions:

Whisk together the broth, sesame oil, rice vinegar and cornstarch in a large bowl. Set aside.

In a wok, heat the cooking oil over high heat until it shimmers.

Add the ginger, garlic and pork and stir-fry for about 1 minute.

Place the carrots and stir-fry for about 1 minute.

Pour the broth mixture to the wok and stir until the cornstarch dissolves entirely and the broth comes to a boil.

Then put the bok choy and allow to cook for about 1 minute.

Toss the shrimp, followed by the scallops and fish. Cook for about 2 minutes.

Garnish with the scallions and serve warm.

Nutrition: calories: 394 carbs: 11g protein: 29g fat: 28g phosphorus: 316mg potassium: 745mg sodium: 252mg

Chicken and vegetables stir-fry soup

Preparation time: 10 minutes

Cooking time: 10 minutes

Serving: 4

Ingredients:

1 pound (454 g) ground or finely chopped chicken

1 cup chopped bok choy

1 medium onion, diced

1 bell pepper (any color), cut into ½-inch pieces

3 quarts meat or vegetable broth

2 garlic cloves, crushed and chopped

4 scallions, cut into ¼-inch pieces

2 tbsps. Cooking oil

1 tbsp. Ginger, crushed and chopped

Fresh chopped herbs such as cilantro, mint, parsley, or basil, for garnish

Directions:

In a wok, heat the cooking oil over high heat until it shimmers.

Add the garlic, ginger, chicken, onion, and bell pepper and stir-fry for about 1 minute.

Place the bok choy and stir-fry for about 30 seconds.

Pour the broth and bring to a gentle boil.

Squeeze the scallions to bruise them, while sprinkling them into the soup.

Garnish with chopped herbs and serve.

Nutrition: calories: 127 fat: 10g carbohydrates: 8g protein: 4g

Healthy Pork and Egg Drop Soup

Preparation time: 10 minutes

Cooking Time: 15 minutes

Serving: 4

Ingredients:

1 pound (454 g) ground pork

4 eggs, beaten

1 cup chopped bok choy

1 ounce (28 g) dried, sliced shiitake or tree ear mushrooms

¼ cup cornstarch

4 scallions, cut into ½-inch pieces

2 garlic cloves, crushed and chopped

3 quarts plus 1¼ cups vegetable or meat broth, divided

1 tbsp. Ginger, crushed and chopped

Directions:

Mix 1 cup of the broth with the cornstarch and stir to form a slurry. Keep aside.

In a wok, boil ¼ cup of the broth over high heat.

Add the pork, garlic and ginger and cook for about 1 minute.

Pour the remaining 3 quarts broth and the mushrooms to the wok. Bring to a boil.

Toss the cornstarch slurry into the boiling broth until the broth thickens.

Stir the broth in one direction while drizzling the beaten eggs into the wok.

Add the bok choy to the broth and let cook for about 30 seconds.

Squeeze the scallions to bruise them, while sprinkling them into the soup.

Serve hot.

Nutrition: Calories: 127 Fat: 10g Carbohydrates: 8g Protein: 4g

Hot and Sour Beef and Carrot Soup

Preparation time: 10 minutes

Cooking Time: 20 minutes

Serving: 4

Ingredients:

1 pound (454 g) shaved steak

1 medium carrot, julienned

1 medium onion, cut into 1-inch pieces

1 cup chopped bok choy

4 ounces (113 g) mushrooms, sliced

¼ cup rice vinegar

3 quarts vegetable or meat broth

2 garlic cloves, crushed and chopped

2 tbsps. Cooking oil

1 tbsp. Crushed chopped ginger

1 tsp. Hot sesame oil

Directions:

In a wok, heat the cooking oil over high heat until it shimmers.

Add the garlic, ginger and carrot and stir-fry for about 30 seconds.

Then place the onion and mushrooms and stir-fry for about 30 seconds.

Pour in the broth, sesame oil and rice vinegar and bring to a boil.

Put the bok choy and steak and stir for about 30 seconds.

Serve hot.

Nutrition: Calories: 127 Fat: 10g Carbohydrates: 8g Protein: 4g

Coconut Oatmeal Cookies

Preparation time: 10 minutes

Cooking Time: 20 minutes

Serving: 4

Ingredients:

1 teaspoon baking powder

1 teaspoon baking soda

1 teaspoon vanilla

2 cups flour

2 cups rolled oats

2 large eggs

1/2 cup butter

1/2 cup shortening

1 cup brown sugar, packed or 2 tablespoons molasses

1 cup flaked coconut

1 cup raisins (optional) or 1 cup chocolate chips (optional)

1 cup white sugar

Directions

In a mixing dish, combine the butter, sugars, and shortening. Incorporate the eggs. Blend in the vanilla extract. Set aside.

In a separate dish, combine the dry ingredients. After all of the ingredients have been combined, add the coconut. Combine the wet and dry ingredients and place them on a cookie sheet previously coated with cooking spray.

Cook for 10 minutes on a rack in a wok, or until golden brown.

Nutrition: Calories 90.4, Fat: 4g, Net Carbs: 12.7g, Protein: 1.3g

Ginger Egg Drop Soup

Preparation time: 10 minutes

Cooking Time: 20 minutes

Serving: 4

Ingredients:

2 large eggs, lightly beaten

4 cups low-sodium chicken broth

2 peeled fresh ginger slices, each about the size of a quarter

2 scallions, thinly sliced, for garnish

2 garlic cloves, peeled

3 tbsps. Water

2 tbsps. Cornstarch

2 tsps. Light soy sauce

1 tsp. Sesame oil

Directions:

In a wok over high heat, combine the broth, garlic, ginger, and light soy and bring to a boil. Reduce to a simmer and cook for about 5 minutes. Remove the ginger and garlic and discard.

Mix the cornstarch and water in a small bowl and stir the mixture into the wok. Lower the heat to medium-high and stir for 30 seconds, until the soup thickens.

Reduce the heat to a simmer. Dip a fork into the beaten eggs and then drag it through the soup, slowly stirring as you go. Continue to dip the fork into the egg and drag it through the soup to make the egg threads. Once all the egg has been added, simmer the soup undisturbed for a few moments to set the eggs. Drizzle in the sesame oil and scoop the soup into serving bowls. Sprinkle with the scallions and serve.

Nutrition: calories: 184 fat: 15g carbohydrates: 1g protein: 12g

Healthy Pork Congee

Preparation time: 10 minutes

Cooking Time: 60 minutes

Serving: 4

Ingredients:

¾ cup jasmine rice, rinsed and drained

6 ounces (170 g) ground pork

2 garlic cloves, minced

10 cups water

2 tbsps. Vegetable oil

1 tbsp. Light soy sauce, plus more for serving

2 tsps. Peeled minced fresh ginger

2 tsps. Shaoxing rice wine

2 tsps. Cornstarch

1 tsp. Kosher salt

Directions:

In a heavy-bottomed pot over high heat, bring the water to a boil. Stir in the salt and rice and reduce the heat to a simmer. Cover and cook, stirring frequently, for about 1½ hours, until the rice has turned to a soft porridge-like consistency.

While the congee is cooking, stir together the garlic, ginger, light soy, rice wine, and cornstarch in a medium bowl. Add the pork and let it marinate for about 15 minutes.

Heat a wok over high heat until a drop of water sizzles and evaporates on contact. Add the vegetable oil and swirl to coat the base of the wok evenly. Place the pork and stir-fry, tossing and breaking up the meat, for about 2 minutes. To get some caramelization, cook for another 1 to 2 minutes without stirring.

Top the congee with the stir-fried pork and serve hot.

Nutrition: calories: 184 fat: 15g carbohydrates: 1g protein: 12g

Hot and Sour Noodle with Pork Soup

Preparation time: 10 minutes

Cooking Time: 8 minutes

Serving: 4

Ingredients:

8 ounces (227 g) dry vermicelli glass noodles

½ pound (227 g) ground pork

4 eggs, cracked into a bowl with yolks unbroken

1 cup chopped bok choy

1 medium carrot, julienned

¼ cup rice vinegar

3 quarts meat or vegetable broth

2 garlic cloves, crushed and chopped

1 scallion, cut into ½-inch pieces

2 tbsps. Cooking oil

1 tbsp. Ginger, crushed and chopped

1 tsp. Hot sesame oil

Directions:

In a wok, heat the cooking oil over high heat until it shimmers.

Add the garlic, ginger, pork, and carrot and stir-fry for about 1 minute.

Pour the broth, noodles, sesame oil and rice vinegar and bring to a boil.

Add the eggs into the boiling broth without breaking the yolks and poach for about 1 minute.

Scatter the bok choy into the soup and allow it to cook for 1 minute.

Sprinkle with the scallion and serve with one egg in each bowl.

Nutrition: calories: 184 fat: 15g carbohydrates: 1g protein: 12g

Ice Cream Cake Batter

Preparation time: 10 minutes

Cooking Time: 30 minutes

Serving: 4

Ingredients:

1 teaspoon pure of vanilla extract

2 cups of heavy cream, well chilled

2/3 cup cake mix

3/4 cup granulated sugar

1 cup whole milk, well chilled

Directions

To begin, place the ice cream maker container in the freezer. Whisk together the milk and granulated sugar until the sugar is completely dissolved in a wok. Blend in a thick, creamy sauce. Blend in the vanilla extract. Mix in the cake mix until all lumps are gone. Pour the ingredients into a freezer bowl and combine for about half-hour until thick.

Remove ice cream from the freezer bowl and place it in a separate container.

Place the freezer bowl and the ice cream in the freezer.

Nutrition: Calories 360, Fat: 19g, Net Carbs: 44g, Protein: 5g

Lotus Root Salad

Preparation time: 10 minutes

Cooking Time: 20 minutes

Serving: 4

Ingredients:

1 and 1/2 tablespoons soy sauce

1 and 1/2 tablespoons white vinegar

1 pound fresh lotus root

1/4 teaspoon Asian chili oil (optional)

2 tablespoons chopped cilantro

1/2 tablespoon sesame oil

Toasted black sesame seeds or sesame seeds

Directions

To begin, bring three quarts of water to boil in a kettle. Rinse all lotus roots well.

Trim, then remove the two ends of the bulb after that. Remember to peel out the skin. Cut the root into thick slices diagonally and immerse them in a water bowl with vinegar.

Drain the roots and set them in a wok of boiling water. Take the wok off the heat and cover it. Allow for a 5-minute rest period. Drain and rinse thoroughly. Place them in a shallow basin after drying them.

Combine the soy sauce, cilantro, chili oil, vinegar, and sesame oil in a mixing bowl. Pour the topping on your lotus roots and sprinkle the sesame seeds on top.

Nutrition: Calories 496.9, Fat: 8.3g, Net Carbs: 64.9g, Protein: 44g

Parsley and Chinese Cabbage Salad

Preparation time: 10 minutes

Cooking Time: 20 minutes

Serving: 4

Ingredients:

1 tablespoon ginger, grated

1 tablespoon whole grain mustard

1/4 cup mayonnaise

2 cups fresh parsley, roughly chopped

4 cups Chinese cabbage, shredded

4 tablespoons reserved pineapple extract

1/2 red onion, thinly sliced

1 cup chopped pineapple

1 cup shredded carrot

Salt and freshly ground black pepper, to taste

Directions

Combine the thinly chopped red onion, shredded carrot, pineapple, cabbage, and parsley in a Ziploc bag. In a wok, sauté all of them. Allow cooling after sealing the bag.

Combine the ginger, whole grain mustard, mayonnaise, pineapple extract, salt, and ground black pepper in a mixing bowl. Allow cooling before covering.

Pour the topping into a Ziploc bag and stir well.

Nutrition: Calories 104.8, Fat: 8.1g, Net Carbs: 7g, Protein: 2.8g

Peach Fresh Cobbler

Preparation time: 10 minutes

Cooking Time: 20 minutes

Serving: 4

Ingredients:

1 and 1/2 cups sugar, divided

1 teaspoon baking powder

2 pinches of salt

3 cups peaches, peeled, pitted, and sliced

1/2 cup margarine

1/2 cup milk

1/2 cup water

1/2 teaspoon vanilla

1 cup flour

Directions

First, grease the wok with cooking spray and line it with peaches.

Combine milk, half a cup of sugar, and vanilla with margarine, flour, salt, and baking powder in a mixing bowl. Blend until completely smooth.

Pour it over the fruit after that. Combine 1 cup of sugar and 1 cup of water in a mixing bowl and pour it on top of the batter.

Preheat the wok and cook for 60 minutes.

Nutrition: Calories 235.9, Fat: 8.9g, Net Carbs: 42.2g, Protein: 2.1g

Chapter 9: Snacks and sweets Recipes

Broccoli Fritters Recipe

Preparation time: 25 minutes

Cooking Time: 15 minutes

Serving: 4

Ingredients:

Chopped garlic, two tsp.

Green onions, three tbsp.

Broccoli, two cups

Chopped fresh dill, two tbsp.

Vegetable oil, as required

Cumin spice, two tbsp.

Salt to taste

Gram flour, two cups

Chopped onions, two tbsp.

Water, as required

Directions

Mix all the ingredients together.

Heat the oil in a large pan.

Make small fritters and fry them.

When the fritters are golden brown dish them out.

Serve them with your preferred dip.

Your dish is ready to be served.

Nutrition: Calories 260, Fat: 8g, Net Carbs: 44g, Protein: 30g

Buffalo Cauliflower Bites Recipe

Preparation time: 10 minutes

Cooking Time: 10 minutes

Serving: 4

Ingredients:

Asian Sesame oil, two tbsp.

Chopped garlic, two tsp.

Green onions, three tbsp.

Cauliflower florets, two cups

Chopped shallots, two tbsp.

Vegetable oil, two tbsp.

Soy sauce, two tbsp.

Salt to taste

Black pepper to taste

Buffalo sauce, two cups

Chopped onions, two tbsp.

Directions

In a wok, add oil and heat it.

Add in the cauliflower florets and let it cook for five minutes.

Remove the florets of cauliflower once they are cooked.

Add the chopped onions to the wok.

Add in the sauces and let them cook.

Once cooked, add in the rest of the ingredients.

Add the cauliflower florets.

Bring to boil and then turn off the flame.

Your dish is ready to be served.

Nutrition: Calories 260, Fat: 8g, Net Carbs: 44g, Protein: 30g

Butternut Squash and Bean Salad

Preparation time: 15 minutes

Cooking Time: 30 minutes

Serving: 4

Ingredients:

2 (15-ounce / 425-g) cans cannellini beans, drained and rinsed

1 cup peeled, seeded, and diced butternut squash

1 cup chopped baby broccoli

3 slices bacon, cooked and crumbled

1 red onion, chopped

¼ cup chicken stock

3 tbsps. Maple syrup, divided

3 tbsps. Olive oil, divided

½ tsp. Dried thyme leaves

Directions:

In a wok over low heat, place the cannellini beans and cook till heated through.

In a wok over medium heat, heat 1 tbsp. Of the olive oil and cook the red onion for 5 minutes.

Add 1 tbsp. Of the maple syrup and stir to combine well. Reduce the heat to medium-low and simmer for 15 minutes, stirring frequently. Turn off the heat and transfer the onion mixture into beans.

In the same wok over medium heat, heat 1 more tbsp. olive oil and cook the butternut squash for 8 minutes. Add 1 tbsp. of the maple syrup and cook for 5 minutes. Remove from the heat and transfer the squash mixture into beans. In the same wok, heat the remaining 1 tbsp. of the olive oil on medium heat and cook the broccoli for 7 minutes. Remove from the heat and transfer the broccoli into beans.

Place the chicken stock into the bean mixture and increase the heat to medium-low.

Toss in the remaining 1 tbsp. of the maple syrup and thyme and bring to a gentle boil.

Simmer till heated completely, stirring slowly. Top with the crumbled bacon.

Nutrition: Calories: 212 Fat: 15.8g Carbohydrates: 12.1g Protein: 8.6g

Rice-Water Sesame Balls

Preparation time: 10 minutes

Cooking time: 40 minutes

Serving:4

Ingredients:

1 c. of sesame seeds, white

1 c. of vegetable oil

4 c. of rice flour

Directions:

Boil some water.

Mix your sugar and rice flour in a bowl.

Gradually pour the boiled water into the mixture.

Knead thoroughly to form a dough.

Cut dough into as many pieces as you desire.

Form these doughs into balls.

Coat these balls in your sesame seeds.

Fry the balls until golden brown on all sides.

Nutrition:

Sodium: 25mg

Fat: 7g

Calories: 150

Carbs: 21g

Vanilla-Coated Walnuts

Preparation time: 10 minutes

Cooking time: 60 minutes

Serving:4

Ingredients:

1 c. of sugar

⅔ c. of oil

2 eggs

1 tsp. of baking powder

1 tsp. of vanilla extract

½ tsp. of salt

1 c. of walnuts

Directions:

The oven should be preheated at 175° F.

Mix the flour, salt, and baking powder thoroughly.

Mix the eggs, oil, and vanilla extract.

Add the flour, salt, and baking powder mixture and mix well.

Pour the walnuts into the mixture.

Bake for 45 minutes.

Nutrition:

Saturated: 6g

Carbohydrate: 25g

Fat: 11g

Sodium: 48g

Vegan Crunch Wrap Recipe

Preparation time: 25 minutes

Cooking Time: 15 minutes

Serving: 4

Ingredients:

Asian Sesame oil, two tbsp.

Chopped garlic, two tsp.

Green onions, three tbsp.

Tortilla wraps, eight

Mixed vegetables, two cups

Chopped fresh dill, two tbsp.

Vegetable oil, two tbsp.

Salt to taste

Directions

Heat a wok and add in the oil.

Add all the cooking ingredients into the wok and cook.

Cook your vegetables until they are soft and tender for five to ten minutes.

Lay the tortilla wraps with the prepared vegetables and fry them in the wok.

Once golden brown, remove it.

Your dish is ready to be served with your preferred dip.

Nutrition: Calories 260, Fat: 8g, Net Carbs: 44g, Protein: 30g

Vegan Mozzarella Sticks Recipe

Preparation time: 25 minutes

Cooking Time: 15 minutes

Serving: 4

Ingredients:

Chopped garlic, two tsp.

Green onions, three tbsp.

Mozzarella sticks, two cups

Chopped fresh dill, two tbsp.

Vegetable oil, as required

Cumin spice, two tbsp.

Salt to taste

All-purpose flour, two cups

Eggs, two

Water, as required

Directions

Mix all the ingredients together.

Heat the oil in a large pan.

Cover the mozzarella sticks with the batter and fry them.

When the sticks are golden brown, dish them out.

Serve them with your preferred dip.

Nutrition: Calories 260, Fat: 8g, Net Carbs: 44g, Protein: 30g

Vegan Potato Veggies Recipe

Preparation time: 25 minutes

Cooking Time: 15 minutes

Serving: 4

Ingredients:

Asian Sesame oil, two tbsp.

Chopped garlic, two tsp.

Green onions, three tbsp.

Bell pepper strips, half cup

Potatoes, two cups

Chopped fresh dill, two tbsp.

Vegetable oil, two tbsp.

Soy sauce, two tbsp.

Salt to taste

Black pepper to taste

Mushrooms, two cups

Corn, one cup

Corn flour, two tbsp.

Chopped onions, two tbsp.

Directions

Heat a wok on medium flame.

Add in the oil and let it heat up.

Add the onions and cook it until translucent.

Add in the garlic and cook it for two minutes.

Add in the potatoes and cook it for five minutes.

Add in the mushrooms and bell peppers.

Add the soy sauce, salt and pepper into the wok and cook for five minutes.

Add in the corn and water.

Cook the mixture and add the corn flour.

Let the mixture cook for about ten minutes.

Cover the mixture for five minutes.

Cook the potatoes until they turn completely dry.

Add in the sesame oil, green onions and fresh chopped dill on top.

Your dish is ready to be served with any sauce you prefer.

Nutrition: Calories: 49 Fat: 2g Carbohydrates: 4g Protein: 3g

Vegan Zucchini and Cauliflower Fritters Recipe

Preparation time: 10 minutes

Cooking Time: 20 minutes

Serving: 4

Ingredients:

Chopped garlic, two tsp.

Green onions, three tbsp.

Zucchini, two cups

Chopped fresh dill, two tbsp.

Vegetable oil, as required

Cumin spice, two tbsp.

Salt to taste

Gram flour, two cups

Chopped onions, two tbsp.

Cauliflower florets, one cup

Water, as required

Directions

Mix all the ingredients together.

Heat the oil in a large pan.

Make small fritters and fry them.

When the fritters are golden brown, dish them out.

Serve them with your preferred dip.

Your dish is ready to be served.

Nutrition: Calories 260, Fat: 8g, Net Carbs: 44g, Protein: 30g

Conclusion

Thank you for making it to the end.

Chinese cuisine is well-known all around the world. It is well-known not only for its deliciousness, but also for being visually appealing and healthful. Chinese people frequently employ a variety of fresh ingredients when cooking, so each Chinese cuisine is a harmonious combination of scents, flavors, and colors. It's the combo that makes you feel like you're eating a vibrant painting rather than a regular food.

In general, we keep foods fresh and eat them without cooking to preserve their colors and nutrients. Chinese folks are unique. They may keep the color and nutritional value of food even after cooking. Their trick is just cooking at extremely high temperatures in a short period of time. To cook successfully, they devote close attention to the intricate procedure and equipment involved. They employ specialized equipment known as "Wok."

Wok has played such an essential role in Chinese daily life since then. Wok is now found not just in Chinese family kitchens, but also in kitchens from all over the world, thanks to its incredible benefits.

Nowadays, the wok is utilized for a wide range of different dinners all around the world. The majority of the woks are made of carbon steel, which mulls over them. Clearly, Asian food preparation is heavily reliant on the wok, but the wok has a wide range of applications.

We have spent time and effort studying your needs and have developed a wealth of information and recipes to guide you through the process of enjoying your fantastic delicacies.

The wok is a beautiful utensil that has been used for a long time in diverse dishes all around the world. Wok frying has a significant impact on various cooking techniques. In this book, we looked at the numerous plans that evolved from an assortment of dishes that have been cooked in a wok since ancient times. Using a wok has been considered as straightforward and helpful in organizing large food groups in a short timeline and layout.

ENJOY YOUR WOK RECIPES

DOWNLOAD HERE
THE 4 EBOOK BONUS
and
COLOR VERSION OF THE BOOK

Or copy and paste this url:

https://bit.ly/wok4bonusjillyang

Printed in Great Britain
by Amazon

17661576R00066